Dictionary of Children's Clothes

1700s to Present

Dictionary of Children's Clothes

1700s to Present

Noreen Marshall

V&A Publishing

For Dr Marshall, Wren Ayers and Sgt Oldman, in correct attire, of course

First published by V&A Publishing, 2008

V&A Publishing
Victoria and Albert Museum
South Kensington
London SW7 2RL

Distributed in North America by Harry N. Abrams, Inc., New York

ISBN 978 1 851 77547 7
Library of Congress Control Number
2008924017

10 9 8 7 6 5 4 3 2 1
2012 2011 2010 2009 2008

A catalogue record of this book is available from the British Library.

Designed by Holmes Wood
Edited by David Hallworth

New V&A photography by Pip Barnard, V&A Photographic Studio
Line drawings by Leonie C. Davis

Front jacket: Kenzo baby suit. French, 1990–99 (V&A: B.243[1–4]–2000)
Back jacket: Boy's suit. Scottish, 1820–30 (V&A: T.144[A,B]–1962)
Frontispiece: Children playing leapfrog, by Alec Brooking, 1975–85 (V&A: B.21–1998)

Printed in China

V&A Publishing
Victoria and Albert Museum
South Kensington
London SW7 2RL
www.vam.ac.uk

Contents

Introduction
300 Years of Children's Clothes

One of the most frequent comments on childhood in the past is that children were dressed as miniature adults, even as recently as the 1950s. This overlooks the fact that changes in clothing are complex and inconsistent, in children's garments no less than in adults', and are almost always considered subjectively.

Some similarity between the clothing of children and adults is inevitable, since there are few garments and no colours which are exclusive to childhood. This perceived similarity may even be why children have acquired near invisibility to many who look at paintings, sculpture or photographs, and either fail to see children at all, or see them as of no consequence. This is all the more ironic as the corollary for many people is that these 'miniature adults' would also have lived miniature adult lives, which was certainly not the case for the majority.

We have lost the ability to read many of the clues visible to our predecessors. An adult looking at a child in any past era would have no doubt that this was a child, quite apart from any question of size, and would react accordingly. Their eyes would recognize childhood markers such as leading strings, gender indicators, pinafores, muckinders, the fastening of some garments, and young boys in dresses.

Some of the elements that make the clothes of the past look unfamiliar to our eyes are there for a practical reason, such as the use of aprons and pinafores to keep clothes clean when there were no washing machines or modern detergents; the wearing of hats and caps at all times was thought to prevent illness by keeping the head warm; and the wearing of corsets was (ironically) relied upon to support the back and the digestive organs. Our eyes are drawn mainly to what we remain able to understand, namely the similarities to adult dress.

It is also easy to come to the conclusion that the children of any era before our own were less benignly dressed, which probably says more about changing attitudes to childhood than anything about life in the past. This does at least mean that in all the hand-wringing about the quality of children's lives in the 21st century, and myopia about golden ages of childhood, nobody is suggesting a return to corsets, starch and heavy layers of garments.

But we could at least try to distinguish between our own prejudices and those of the period we are considering. 'Current Modes for Children' in the dressmaking periodical *Myra's Journal* (1 August 1889) begins:

Mamma: 'Who are those
extraordinary-looking
children?'
Effie: 'The Cimabue
Browns, Mamma. They're
Aesthetic, you know.'
Mamma: 'So I should
imagine. Do you know
them to speak to?'
Effie: 'Oh *Dear* no,
Mamma – they're most
exclusive. Why, they put
out their tongues at us if
we only *look* at them!'

'The everyday dresses worn by children, whether at home or at the
sea-side, are so simply made that they call for neither description nor
illustration.' This comment stretches credulity to its utmost, even
bearing in mind that fashion plates and magazines frequently showed
clothing in unrealistically elaborate forms, and that the reality was
more straightforward.

There have always been critics of fashion, but few in any era would
have the courage (or the clarity of vision) to argue along the lines of
a similarly dated piece by 'The Lady Dressmaker' in *The Girls' Own
Paper* (1887):

> Some day, when we progress towards the acquirement of common
> sense, how we shall look back to many a foolish opinion and childish
> fashion which we have erected into a Juggernaut car to make our lives
> wretched, and to ruin our health and spirits, merely because we 'must do
> as other people do'. Tight boots and pointed toes, tight stays, large dress
> improvers and huge horse-hair pads, will all be smiled at as foolish, and
> even wicked folly, when we know better in the far future.

Whether or not one entirely agrees with the statement that 'It would
never have been possible in Victorian times to appeal to the children,
for example, when selling merchandise, for they had no say in the matter'
(*The Children's Outfitter*, January 1938), children in the past were
certainly dressed more to adult expectation and convention, including
some notable eccentricities. In the 1880s and 1890s the writer Edith
Nesbit not only dressed her daughters in aesthetic clothing, such as she
wore herself, favouring colours such as apricot and 'old gold', but extended
her individualistic ideas to their underwear. The young daughters (born

between 1905 and 1910) of the artist Eric Gill were expected to wear 'the right and proper dress for a virgin and a Catholic' (unfashionable and hand woven, it seems), as his biographer Fiona MacCarthy expresses it. While it might be expected that the children of artists and writers were among those who suffered most in this context, this was far from always being the case, and other parents also had their foibles.

Ida Gandy (born 1885) recorded that while 'Other children sported petticoats and white drawers – we wore only knickers to match our frocks. I remember Aunt Louisa unpacking my clothes and mourning over the solitary petticoat and drawers that had been included for "a special occasion"'. Their mother evidently preferred 'dashing and original clothes' and applied some of the same principles to her daughters' garments, although her dismissal of petticoats did not extend to corsetry.

> The sight of her great black whalebone stays is one of my earliest
> recollections ... we had been taught that a small waist was an absolute
> necessity for a well-dressed woman, so we meekly submitted to the
> preposterous stays in which our own young bodies were encased at far
> too early an age. When Aunt Selina ... ventured a protest, she was met
> by the unanswerable argument that my father entirely approved.
> (I. Gandy, Staying With the Aunts, 1963)

Clothes were not only generally less comfortable to wear than is now the case, but far more of a burden to the wearer, not just literally in the forms of weight and constriction, but also in terms of the worry they could cause.

When more formal clothing was standard, it could be a considerable cause of anxiety to achieve the correct look in the first place, and to keep the garments in good condition thereafter. Apart from the labour-intensive processes of the laundering of clothing, until the early decades of the 20th century many fabrics were not colour-fast in water, and also faded with exposure to light. With so many difficulties in the cleaning of clothes, any stain, damage or dirt was potentially the ruin of the garment. Gwen Raverat (born 1885) recounts how an evening dress which she hated in her teens was written off:

> I upset a whole dish of spinach into my lap ... and I had on my best
> green satin evening dress, very smart and tight and shiny. I mopped away
> at the mess with my long white kid gloves, and made it much worse ...
> Oh dear, Oh dear, how I did wish to fall down dead that very instant!
> But it was a horrible dress anyhow; I had been allowed no choice in
> colour or make, and I was glad when it was found to be spoilt for ever.
> (G. Raverat, Period Piece: A Cambridge Childhood, 1954)

*East End Girl doing
the Lambeth Walk,*
by Bill Brandt
Gelatin silver print, 1939
V&A: PH.28–1978

She also records how as an Edwardian teenager she would spend up to an hour brushing the mud from the hem of her floor-length winter skirt, and that was after stitching 'brush braid' all round the edge to collect the worst of it and stop it getting on to the rest of the fabric.

What is fair to say is that the progression of fashion is tidal, and that in the process, children's clothing sometimes resembles adult garments closely, and at other times scarcely at all. The roles may also be reversed, when adult clothing takes on a more childlike appearance (consider the 1800s, the 1920s, the 1960s...), sometimes even following where the children lead. We have perhaps now reached a less compartmentalized stage where everyone dresses in what is deemed appropriate: 'adult' clothing for formal occasions, and increasingly for work and school, with 'childlike' garments for casual wear and informal occasions such as holidays and sporting activities.

Portrait miniature
of Richard Whitmore
aged three, by
Bernard Lens III
Watercolour on ivory,
1718
V&A: P.13–1971

Portrait miniature of
Katherine Whitmore,
by Bernard Lens III
Watercolour on ivory,
1724
V&A: P.14–1971

The clothing of 18th-century children was almost as different as it could be from anything worn by children with any regularity today. The key concept of the clothing of the era was that of formality of appearance: males commonly in coats, even indoors (the shirt was still an item of underwear), and females, invariably corseted, with numerous layers of petticoat and skirt. The poor, including the children, also wore formal garments – those that had become shabby, damaged or outmoded and thus discarded by wealthier persons. For centuries, children's clothing had been particularly slow to change its elements, however much this or that shape or cut became fashionable and then outmoded in its turn. For much of the 18th and 19th centuries, children still dressed to a formula which, say, a 16th-century child would have recognized, in garments which clearly followed on from those at the end of the 17th century: chemise, stays, stockings, garters, shoes, petticoats, pocket, dress, cap and apron for a girl; shirt, stockings, shoes, some equivalent of trousers, and a jacket for a boy; swaddling (long bands of fabric wrapped firmly about the body and limbs) for a baby. A boy under six or seven years of age would also have worn a dress and some of the garments associated with it (including, in some cases, stays and pockets). This again is an arrangement that would have been familiar to a child 200 years earlier. Adults' and children's clothing was quite close stylistically, although even so there were some crucial differences for younger children, notably young boys' dresses, and back-fastening garments and leading strings. During the early decades of the 18th century, babies generally wore swaddling, a practice which dated back to ancient times, and was familiar not only from the depictions of children on memorial brasses and tombs of the previous 150 years, but also from the Bible: '… and she brought forth her first born son,

and wrapped him in swaddling clothes, and laid him in a manger...'
(Luke 2:7). The concept is evidently there in the original Greek: '... she
swathed him and laid him in a manger...' (A. Marshall, *The Interlinear
Greek-English New Testament: The Nestle Greek Text with a literal
English Translation,* 1958).

A baby's swaddling was not, as at first sight, a matter of wrapping
it in nothing but bands of fabric. It was normally worn with a set
of separate garments:

• A linen nappy or tail clout [cloth], probably in two layers, and perhaps
  with a layer of absorbent material such as sphagnum moss. This was
  a traditional material in some areas, being not only absorbent and
  antiseptic, but reusable. Much more common was an absorbent layer
  of soft rags (in much the same way that menstruating girls and women
  would use them).

• A wide strip of cloth (the binder) around the waist, which would cover
  the navel while it healed, and perhaps hold a dressing in place there.
  Written medical advice about this dates from as early as 1579, when
  Catherine de Medici's physician, Laurent Joubert (1529–83) published
  his *Popular Errors*. He suggested that the navel string (which in his
  experience was left in place to wither after it had been tied off) should
  be placed within a soft cloth dressing so as not to cause discomfort to the
  child. The binder was also thought to support the internal organs.

• A shirt, in many cases still made from squares and rectangles of fabric
  in the traditional way, which neither required pattern pieces nor wasted
  fabric in turnings and curved facings.

• A 'bed', or thick piece of wadding wrapped around the child, the arms
  and legs having been positioned straight and flat with the arms next to
  the body; a layer of wadding could also be pulled up between the legs for
  greater absorbency. This produced the compact shape of the swaddled
  baby, and kept it warm as well making it easier to wrap.

The layers of swaddling bands were sometimes finished off with a
long decorative one, which might be embroidered or woven with a
stripe. Swaddling could also be put on in decorative patterns such as
herringbone, or diagonal lines. In some cases a panel of fabric, the long
bib, was pinned over the front of the body and legs. A substantial bib,
or 'slavering clout' would be added as needed.

A baby would also wear a forehead cloth, tied on at the back and
sometimes of double thickness, to protect the front of the head; then
an under cap (usually plain) and an over cap (often decorated and

more substantial). A stayband – a strip of fabric which crossed the head or fastened to the cap – was pinned on each shoulder to keep the child's head still (ordinary sharp-ended pins were the main method of fastening baby clothes until the invention of the safety pin in the 19th century).

Swaddling was often reduced after a few months, so that the upper chest and arms were free, and in some countries, such as England, dispensed with altogether after four or five months (among other factors, the lower down the social scale a family was, the more likely a child was to be swaddled to some extent). Working mothers were often unable to tend a child or even keep it in view constantly, so swaddling kept it warm, still and free from danger. It also tended to make a baby more placid, and easier to pick up and carry about. Poorer parents were not only more traditional in outlook, but even less likely than the middle classes to be aware of the arguments against the practice. Swaddling at its most basic was by far the cheapest and most practical solution to the clothing of a baby, with few garments to grow out of, and the wrappings adaptable from almost any fabric that could be spared. All levels of society tended to believe, as the Franciscan theologian Bartholomaeus Anglicus wrote (*c.*1230): 'And for tenderness the limbs of the child may easily and soon bow and bend and take diverse shapes. And therefore children's members and limbs are bound with lystes [bandages], and other covenable bonds, that they be not crooked nor evil shapen.'

Well might Dr William Cadogan write in *A Letter to one of the Governors of the Foundling Hospital, by a Physician* (1748):

> But besides the mischief arising from the Weight and Heat of these Swaddling-Cloaths, they are put on so tight, and the Child is so cramp'd by them, that its Bowels have not Room, nor the Limbs any liberty, to act and exert themselves in the free easy manner they ought … This is a very hurtful circumstance, for Limbs that are not used, will never be strong, and such tender Bodies cannot bear much Pressure … I would recommend the following Dress: A little Flannel waistcoat without sleeves, made to fit the body, and tie loosely behind; to which there should be a Petticoat sew'd, and over this a kind of gown of the same Material, or any other, that is light, thin, and flimsy. The Petticoat should not be quite so long as the Child, the Gown a few inches longer; with one Cap only on the head, which may be made double, if it be thought not warm enough. What I mean is, the whole coiffure should be contrived, that it might be put on at once, and neither bind nor press the Head at all: the Linen as usual. This I think would be abundantly sufficient for the Day; laying aside all those Swathes, Bandages, Stays and Contrivances, that are most rediculously used to close and keep the

*Head in its Place and support the Body. As if Nature, exact Nature, had
produced her chief Work, a human Creature, so carelessly unfinish'd,
as to want these idle Aids to make it perfect.*

Anne Buck, in *Costume in the Eighteenth Century*, suggests that people
seem to have been cleaner in general at the end of the 18th century
than at the beginning (although a heavy tax on soap in England
between 1634 and 1853 can't have helped). In many cases this may
have been a question of washing themselves and changing their
underwear; easier than cleaning their outer clothes.

The babies in their layers of swaddling were certainly difficult to keep
clean, and were often changed once a day or even less. Dr Cadogan
spoke up on this issue, too:

> *There is an odd Notion enough entertained about Change, and the
> keeping of Children clean. Some imagine that clean Linnen and fresh
> Cloaths draw, and rob them of their nourishing Juices. I cannot see that
> they do anything more than imbibe a little of that moisture which their
> Bodies exhale. Were it as it is supposed, it would be of service to them;
> since they are always too abundantly supplied, and therefore I think they
> cannot be changed too often, and would have them clean every Day;
> as it would free them from Stinks and Sournesses, which are not only
> offensive, but very prejudicial to the tender State of Infancy.*

Younger girls' dresses had closed fronts, and did up at the back.
They sometimes retained the leading strings of the younger child, even
in their teens, possibly as symbolic of their dependence on their parents.
The open-fronted robe was only appropriate to older girls and adult
women, or in the rare case of a girl appearing at the royal court, when
she would also have worn the wide pannier hoops that were required
as part of female court dress at the time.

Boys of the 18th century wore breeches and coats, which in the most
fashionable instances were almost as close-fitting as the girls' dresses.
For formal wear, boys in society might also shave their hair off and
wear a wig, or at least wear their hair powdered white, as shown in the
portraits of Wolfgang Amadeus Mozart (born 1756) when he was a child
music prodigy touring Europe.

The origin of younger boys wearing dresses may be simply that before
about 1550, both sexes and all ages wore skirted garments: tunics and
gowns. Young children in the medieval and early Tudor period, once
past the age of swaddling, had worn a simple and extremely practical
loose-cut gown or coat, either knitted or made of cloth, and usually with
a round neck and long sleeves.

Other theories include the idea that all children of this age were considered more or less as babies, and so wore the same type of garments; that it was appropriate for the boys to wear skirts because young children were cared for by women rather than men; that it protected the legs of young children if they fell while learning to walk; that it would be easier to change nappies. In fact, the age for breeching suggests that making it easier for young boys to urinate or defecate is perhaps the main explanation. This would be especially true when breeches or trousers had complicated fastenings, which took a long time to undo.

Putting dresses on boys was emphatically not treating them as girls, just as dressing girls in trousers from the 1930s onward was not treating them as boys. And as all young boys wore dresses, they would not have felt conspicuous in skirts, although they undoubtedly looked forward to getting their first trousers and being thought of as more grown up. Rousseau, always perceived as influential with his writings on childhood in *Emile* (1762) but whose ideas parents seldom put into practice in their entirety, was an advocate of dresses, and wrote, 'The best plan is to keep children in frocks [for] as long as possible, and then to provide them with loose clothes'.

The age at which boys acquired their first breeches or trousers varied from about four to about eight years, depending on the period, the location, and the family; although between five and seven seems to have been the most common age. In some eras the trousers were accompanied by a first weapon, for those who could afford it, and a first haircut or wig. Hazel Forsyth, author with Geoff Egan of *Toys, Trifles and Trinkets*, has suggested that the miniature weapons which survive from the 17th and 18th centuries may have been a token alternative.

The far-reaching changes in children's fashions of the 1770s and 1780s – when formal coats, corsetry, dresses and wigs were replaced by trousers and short jackets for boys, and light and simple dresses for girls and the youngest children – were only gradual. Swaddling was almost entirely discontinued in the UK and the USA by the end of the 18th century, although the number of garments used in its place meant that the infant might be said to have exchanged one sort of overdressing for another. However, at a time of high infant mortality (which was the case until some way into the 20th century) most parents and carers were unwilling to accept the word of a physician like Cadogan that 'a new-born Child cannot well be too cool and loose in its Dress; it wants less Cloathing than a grown Person, in proportion; because it is naturally warmer, as appears by the Thermometer'.

Portrait miniature
of an unknown boy
wearing a skeleton suit,
by Richard Cosway
Watercolour on ivory,
1799
V&A: P.7–1941

Portrait miniature
of an unknown girl,
by John Cox Dillman
Engleheart
Watercolour on ivory,
1807
V&A: 413–1907

In this, the children were taking the lead. Adult fashions only changed in the aftermath of the French Revolution of 1789–99. Revolutionary ideology in France required a radical change in the clothing of the whole populace, as the previously established modes of the 18th century were associated with the old pre-revolutionary order under the monarchy. However, portraits of the 1780s showing the Dauphin Louis-Joseph Xavier (1781–9), notably those by Vigée le Brun, invariably show him in the new trousers, not breeches. The French had, as James Laver points out in *A Concise History of Costume*, 'much enthusiasm … for all things English', and the new French fashions for men and boys echoed the clothing of the English country gentleman (or rather their idea of what he wore). Girls' and women's fashions were imaginatively interpreted from the draperies of ancient Greek statues. These fashions became the ideal all over Europe, even in countries with few or no republican aspirations.

The skeleton suit, in which the jacket and trousers buttoned together, was probably the most widely worn version of the new British fashion for short jackets and trousers, certainly as a characteristic garment of younger boys, although at least some of the very youngest continued to wear dresses, probably for practical hygienic reasons. A 1799 engraving of Hoppner's portrait of Lady Anne Lambton with her daughter and three sons shows the youngest boy in a light dress like his young sister's, while their elder brothers wear trousers and short tops.

Dickens used the motif of a skeleton suit in late use, in connection with the abused boy Smike at Dotheboys Hall in *Nicholas Nickleby*, to underline the pathos of his situation:

> *Although he could not have been less than eighteen or nineteen years old, and was tall for that age, he wore a skeleton suit, such as is usually put upon very little boys, and which, though most absurdly short in the arms and legs, was quite wide enough for his attenuated frame … Heaven knows how long he had been there, but he still wore the same linen which he had first taken down; for, round his neck, was a tattered child's frill, only half concealed by a coarse, man's neckerchief.*
> (*The Life and Times of Nicholas Nickelby*, 1839)

Neither girls' white dresses nor white baby robes were worn as constantly as their survival suggests. In both cases, print frocks were often the staple everyday wear in the late years of the 18th century and the early decades of the 19th. White dresses were certainly worn for best, and some even showed the neoclassical influence of French 'chemise' dresses, with narrow skirts and the briefest of bodices, sometimes contrasting this with a characteristically British element such as needleworked 'Dorset wheel' buttons, or Ayrshire whitework embroidery.

Opposite
The children of Elhanan
Bicknell, by S.P. Denning
(detail)
Watercolour, *c.*1842
V&A: P.18–1934

Below
Walking costumes
Fashion plate, 1809
V&A: E.1164–1946

A highly contrasting tendency to the neoclassical was also present in
England, rooted in the English attachment to the past. James Laver
commented that 'When the English ladies flocked over to Paris in 1814
after Napoleon's first abdication, they found to their astonishment that
English and French fashions had notably diverged ... English costume
... was beginning to look 'romantic', with echoes of such Elizabethan
elements as puffed and slashed sleeves' (J. Laver, *A Concise History
of Costume*). As a result, English women apparently gave up their
historically based look and adopted the plainer French styles. The same
was emphatically not to be true of some of their male descendants, or at
least not when below the age of about twelve years. The 'Vandyke' look
had existed in the 18th century, if only as a 'fancy' in portraiture, but
the younger 19th-century boy was sometimes arrayed in a bewildering
number of garments and accessories which more nearly resembled
fancy dress than anything else.

'An Old Clothes Shop,
Seven Dials', by
John Thomson, from
the bound volume
Street Life in London
Woodburytype, 1877–8
V&A: PH.978–1978

The 19th century saw more changes in children's fashion, more variety and more consumer choice than ever before, and one of the greatest areas of innovation and custom was that of underwear. Apart from the later novelties of crinolines, bustles and sock suspenders, the new fashions for underpants and vests (and later combinations) established themselves quickly, especially in the aspiring middle classes. These increasing layers of underclothes sat well with prevailing notions of modesty, and it was also realized that efficient use of underclothing could save a good deal of cleaning of the outer clothes:

> *Every moisture or impurity, should be instantly removed, and as those*
> *parts of the dress which are next to the skin are constantly imbibing*
> *perspirable matter, they should be changed frequently. Indeed, the same*
> *clothes ought never to be kept on for many days together. Away with*
> *finery; but take care that the child is always clean and dry.*
> (*The New Female Instructor*, 1834)

The poor still bought discarded clothes from dealers, and sold them when times were harder than usual, or when they no longer needed them. One reason for the low survival rate of their clothing is that they had neither the space nor the financial security to keep anything for which there was no immediate need. Dickens describes David Copperfield selling first his waistcoat and then his jacket to second-hand clothes dealers to avoid starvation on his runaway journey to his aunt in Chatham:

> *Feeling that I could go but a very little way that day, if I were to reserve*
> *any strength for getting to my journey's end, I resolved to make the sale*
> *of my jacket its principal business. Accordingly, I took the jacket off, that I*
> *might learn to do without it; and carrying it under my arm, began a tour of*
> *inspection of the various slop-shops. It was a likely place to sell a jacket*
> *in; for the dealers in second-hand clothes were numerous, and were,*
> *generally speaking, on the look-out for customers at their shop doors.*
> (*David Copperfield*, 1850)

The 19th century also saw an upsurge in the founding of sewing circles and groups for the charitable provision of clothing for the poor. Some of them were called Dorcas Societies, like the one founded in Douglas, Isle of Man in 1834, following the destruction of bedding and clothes in a recent cholera epidemic that had caused much hardship among the poorer families. Its aim was 'to administer relief to the poor and necessitous of Plain and Necessary Articles of Clothing'. Dorcas was a Biblical character, a seamstress 'full of good works and almsdeeds', who had died and been restored to life by St Peter. 'When he was come, they brought him into the upper chamber: and all the widows stood by him weeping, and shewing the coats and garments which Dorcas made, while she was with them' (Acts 9:39).

Portrait miniature
of the Duke of Reichstadt
as a boy, by J.B. Isabey
Watercolour on ivory,
c.1818
V&A: P.40–1948

In the years between 1800 and 1835, one of Rousseau's pet aversions, the hussar fashions, had a considerable influence on children's clothing. Many children's garments of the period were inspired by the colourful uniforms of the hussar cavalry regiments, with their extravagantly decorative use of braid, tassels, sashes and frogging. Even baby gowns were not immune from densely applied patterns of looped white braid on the bodices and sleeves.

Baby clothes had, in fact, begun the century with the simple enough forms of the chemise dress or the slip dress, accompanied by a dozen or so other items. A typical layette would consist of:

- a binder (a length of fabric wound around the waist to cover the navel and support the waist)
- a linen nappy (towards the end of the century towelling began to be used)
- a pilch or nappy cover, sometimes of waterproof fabric
- a shirt or knitted vest
- two caps
- a bodice
- a barracoat (a warm flannel petticoat, sometimes tied round the feet)
- one or more long petticoats
- a long gown
- a shawl (or a long cape for outdoor wear)
- a bib or pinafore
- socks and shoes

This form of the layette was to last for almost 150 years. Baby garments tended to be passed around families and friends. They were altered and refurbished, and new garments sometimes made to replace those that had worn out, but it was almost unheard of for a baby to have a completely new set of garments.

Portrait of an unknown
child by William Howie
Photographic print, 1860s
V&A: MoC

Sometimes minor changes crept in when new baby gowns were made in the course of the 19th century, such as a lower waist, higher neck and longer sleeves, and from the 1890s, a yoked bodice for a less constricting fit. Sometimes, overhauling the garments for a later generation would result in alterations such as adding longer sleeves or a higher neckline within the existing ones. The thrifty would even combine the elements of several old and damaged or worn-out dresses to make a new one, or shorten a long dress to take the baby clothing into the next (shorter) stage, that of 'shortening' or 'short-coating' (also known simply as 'tucking up'). Mass-production techniques introduced into the textile industry during the 19th century made embroidered and lace trimmings much more affordable and more widely available from drapers' shops. This led to the abandoning of much of the exquisite but labour-intensive embroidery and finishing that had

Master Grierson,
by David Octavius Hill
and Robert Adamson
Salt paper print, *c.*1845
V&A: 67.379

previously characterized infants' clothing, but some examples survive with panels of decorative insertion that are jigsaw-like in their complexity.

The basic colour for baby clothes continued to be white, for a number of reasons. White was symbolic of innocence, it was considered aesthetically more suited to the colouring of so young a child, and it was more easily washed (or boiled, or bleached). Dyes for coloured garments were not necessarily colour-fast, and could even be poisonous (particularly green, which might contain arsenic).

With the slow rate of change in children's fashions, very long gowns for babies continued to be worn, often a full 24 inches or more beyond the feet of the child, which Alison Lurie in *The Language of Clothes* (1983) suggests is a kind of 'sympathetic magic' as it 'anticipates, or perhaps magically ensures, that he or she will outlive the years of high mortality' (by appearing to be taller and therefore older). In this case the change to the shorter clothes which were subsequently worn by a young child could presumably be read as the baby having grown so well as to have passed the early months at an accelerated rate. On the other hand, the apparently illogical practice of putting tucks (usually in children's garments at least nominally to allow for growth) in the skirts of infants' long gowns was most likely to have had a practical cause: to take up some of the excess length. A band of eight tucks could make a difference of some 6 inches, and help to avoid some of the accidents reported when nursery maids – often still children themselves – attempted to carry the baby and tripped over the robes trailing by their feet.

Boy's dress, with
extra sleeves attached
(see also p.214)
Wool, *c.*1850
V&A: T.83 & A,B–1966

The custom of putting the youngest boys in dresses continued, and with it the use of related undergarments, including petticoats and pantalettes. Boys' dresses were often made in stronger colours than those for girls, and sometimes showed a certain amount of exaggeration, particularly in details such as belts, metallic buttons, and tailored appearance, like a red wool dress of about 1850 in the V&A Museum of Childhood collection (pictured left). It has a dramatic red and black colour scheme, with a prominently tasselled cord around the waist, and a pair of (detachable) extra sleeves which, when hooked into place over the short sleeves, change the appearance of the garment completely, making it resemble much more closely the tunics that older boys were wearing with trousers at this date. This appears to have been a particularly popular and comfortable fashion.

At the same time, girls – some of whom had, when younger, worn the lightweight, high-waisted frocks of the late 18th and earlier 19th centuries – now had to accustom themselves to heavier fabrics, tight

Mourning dresses
Fashion plate, 1809
V&A: E.2799–1888

lacing and a lower waist. Could the crinoline frame, which stopped the weight of their petticoats gathering around their legs, have been sufficient compensation?

The wearing of mourning clothes was of particular importance in the 19th and early 20th centuries. At its height, the convention supported a number of firms which specialized in mourning for the whole family, including the servants. Jay's and Peter Robinson's, whose principal Mourning Warehouses were situated in Regent Street, also provided travelling dressmakers and milliners at no extra charge, and Jay's would even conduct the funeral itself (*Myra's Journal*, 1 March 1887 and 1 May 1885).

The Workwoman's Guide of 1838 advises:

> *Young persons, or those in mourning for young persons, frequently wear a good deal of white, as for instance, white ribbons, handkerchiefs, and white gloves sewed with black. Very young children, only wear white frocks and black ribbons.*
> *The following observations may be found useful in some cases, though they should be received with allowance, according to the circumstances in which the individuals are placed.*
> *For a husband or wife, one to two years*
> *For a parent, six months or a year*
> *For children, if above ten years old, from six months to a year; below that age from three to six months*
> *For an infant, six weeks and upwards*
> *Brothers or sisters six to eight months; uncles and aunts three to six months*
> *Cousins, uncles, aunts related by marriage, six weeks to three months*
> *More distant relations or friends, three weeks upwards*

What was, or was not, acceptable mourning wear in various circumstances was well documented, although even at its height there was a widespread feeling that deep mourning for the youngest children was not really appropriate.

Queen Victoria was most emphatic about wearing full black mourning for family members, and wrote to her eldest daughter Victoria, Empress of Germany, 'You must promise me that if I should die your child or children and those around you should mourn; this really must be, for I have such strong feelings on the subject' (*Dearest Child: Letters between Queen Victoria and the Princess Royal 1858–1861*).

When the husband of the Queen's half sister Feodora died in 1860, the Queen had no hesitation in putting her own three-year-old daughter into mourning, commenting, 'Darling Beatrice looks lovely in her black silk and crepe dress'.

Far more typical of mourning clothes for the younger age group is the set of garments in the collections of the National Trust Museum of Childhood: a set of boy's mourning garments for his mother who died in 1871. At this point he was aged six and still in skirts, and his first mourning garments were white dresses trimmed with black braid. Once he graduated to the wearing of trousers, probably later in the same year, deeper mourning clothes were considered appropriate, and a black velvet suit was provided. This eventually lessened to the half mourning of a white suit with black trimming.

The families who had sewing and mending skills, or who could afford to pay for them, were at a great advantage. When sewing machines became widely available in the 1860s and 1870s, many became treasured family possessions for their usefulness, although some of the thriftier sewers disliked them, saying that they marked the fabric more in making the stitch than a hand-held needle would, and so made it harder to reuse a garment to make something else. They were also of little or no use in darning or 'invisible' mending:

> sewing machines, wonderful though they are, are no match for the cunning devices of well-trained fingers. A working man's wife especially needs this cleverness, for the greater part of her needlework will consist of that 'fine art of mending', which sewing-machines cannot undertake at all. (*Domestic Economy: A Class-Book for Girls*, 1897)

The extent to which clothes were used and reused, and also dyed and even turned inside out and re-stitched – even in wealthier families – is staggering. There was a plethora of printed instruction on how to make clothing, and paper patterns for cutting out the different parts of the garments, especially with the growth of printed periodicals. Samuel Beeton is credited with producing the earliest dress patterns in a magazine, *The Englishwoman's Domestic Magazine*, from 1852.

The Maths Lesson,
by an unknown artist
Oil on canvas, 1840–50
V&A: B.2–2007

Wearers were also much more conscious of the fabrics from which their clothes were made, often referring to 'my grey alpaca' or 'my blue merino', for example. 'Miss Petingill drew back her head, perched the spectacles on her nose, and went to work again on Katy's plaid alpaca, which had two immense zigzag rents across the middle of the front breadth...' (S. Coolidge, *What Katy Did*, set *c*.1864).

The awareness of fabric types also assisted in their cleaning. The ability to do the laundry well was of the greatest importance. Victorian ingenuity in cleaning ranged from the use of cornflour to refresh white lawn to gin for the removal of grease spots. Families strove to turn out their children in clean clothes, especially the white garments, as a sign that they were respectable.

Boy's sailor suit,
detail from a fashion
plate in Portrait Gallery
of British Costume,
published with *The Tailor
and Cutter* by John
Williamson, July 1873
V&A: E.857–1946

*It was before the days of patent soaps and washing powders, and
much hard rubbing was involved. There were no washing coppers,
and the clothes had to be boiled in the big cooking pots over the fire …
the clothes, well blued, were hung on the lines or spread on the hedges.
In wet weather they had to be dried indoors, and no one who has not
experienced it can imagine the misery of living for several days with
a firmament of drying clothes on lines overhead.*
(*Lark Rise to Candleford*, Flora Thompson's autobiographical novel
about her childhood in rural Oxfordshire in the 1880s)

Older boys' clothes in the 19th century were quite sober by comparison
with the fanciful outfits of their younger contemporaries. The Scotch
or Highland suit was a favourite fashion for boys in the second half
of the 19th century and beyond. Despite the disapproval of clothes
reformers like the writer and feminist Ada Ballin, it was remarkable
for its widespread appeal and sheer longevity (the two suits in the V&A
Museum of Childhood collection come from the years 1870 and 1918).
The sailor suit was similarly long lived, its eventual popularity perhaps
easy to understand in an island with a long naval tradition.

Perhaps the most extreme version of such clothing was the Fauntleroy
suit, the 17th-century-inspired outfit of velvet with a lace collar worn
by the hero of Frances Hodgson Burnett's bestselling novel *Little Lord
Fauntleroy* (1886). But the fashions for the Scotch or Highland suit and
the sailor suit were no less a fantasy than the faux aristocratic appeal
of the Fauntleroy outfit. The kilt and the use of clan tartans in this
context seemingly required no Scottish ancestry of any kind, nor the
sailors any naval predecessors.

Over a century after William Cadogan's 1748 *Letter to one of the
Governors of the Foundling Hospital*, Ada Ballin passionately believed
that children were still dressed wrongly. She pulled no punches in her
comments in *The Science of Dress*:

*In choosing materials for clothing, care must be taken to avoid weight, while
securing warmth, and above all, they should be inexpensive and strong,
so that the child may not suffer from being forbidden healthy play lest its
clothes should be spoiled. It must be a poor sort of mother's love – and
yet it is a very common one – which prefers the welfare of the clothes to
that of the child. If a woman wants a block to set fine clothes on, let her
get one made of wood or wax, but not turn her little boy or girl into one …
In England more than half of all the children die under twelve years of
age, and they die chiefly from insufficient clothing … From one point of
view only can anything be said in its favour, and that is, allowing there are
already too many people in the world, it will be an advantage to get rid of
as many of the weakest of the newcomers as possible.*

Opposite
Justin Laczkovic
wearing a Scotch suit
Sepia albumen print, 1883
V&A: B.82(27)–1995

Street Fountain, Battersea,
by Paul Martin
Photograph, *c.*1890
V&A: 2908–1937

Mrs Ballin was aiming at vanity, fashion, and conspicuous consumption (visibly expensive possessions) on the part of parents in general, and mothers in particular.

> *The perverted reason of woman makes her, in accordance with a foolish fashion, cut her baby's clothes low in the neck, and tie up its already short sleeves so that 'it shall look pretty'.*

Some of the insufficient clothing from which children suffered at this date was not, of course, due to anything other than the appalling conditions among the increasing numbers of poor families in late Victorian and Edwardian Britain, particularly in the big cities. Too often, a family of ten or more children could end up on or below the breadline if the main wage earner, usually the father, died or was unable to work. The only organized social assistance in all areas was the workhouse, where conditions were as grim as Dickens portrayed them in *Oliver Twist* in 1838. There had always been children growing up in poverty, but the problem was apparently increasing to the point where some in authority seriously argued that such persons should be forcibly prevented from reproducing.

In 1888, the writer Edith Nesbit instituted an annual Christmas treat for poor children in Deptford, when among other things each received a useful item of clothing made during working parties by Nesbit's circle of friends. The girls mainly received a dress or flannel petticoat, and the boys a woollen comforter, but one year her brother-in-law, 'who had an interest in a Manchester cloth-manufacturing firm, provided yards of blue corduroy suitable for trouser-making. That year every woman who helped remembered sewing up interminable pairs of navy blue corduroy pants [trousers] – for many of the poor children were inadequately clothed' (J. Briggs, *A Woman of Passion: The Life of E. Nesbit*). But the scheme was a victim of its own success: ten years on the original twenty children had become a thousand, and the idea was given up.

Costume historians generally agree that children's clothing of the period 1890 to 1910 was immensely liberating, although the actual garments worn by babies changed very little (and in some cases became even more elaborate). But while there was no doubt that the increasingly available sailor suits, sandals, jerseys, smocks, combinations and liberty bodices were easier to wear than many of the older styles of garments had been, and helped to lessen the weight, tightness and constriction of children's clothing, it seemed that the children who experienced them didn't always see it that way. For one thing, the garments were often still made of heavy fabrics and worn in numerous layers:

> ... *all girls' clothing of the period appeared to be designed by their elders on the assumption that decency consisted in leaving exposed to the sun and air no part of the human body that could possibly be covered with flannel.*
> (Vera Brittain, born 1893, *Testament of Youth*)

> *In Narnia your good clothes were never your uncomfortable ones. They knew how to make things that felt beautiful as well as looking beautiful in Narnia: and there was no such thing as starch or flannel or elastic to be found from one end of the country to the other.*
> (C.S. Lewis, born 1898, *The Last Battle*)

The biggest shock in these matters was probably experienced by the children who were sent to the UK from their parents' homes in countries such as China or India, where they had often worn far lighter clothes, had native servants to take care of their laundry and mending, and in a few cases had even worn more relaxed garments after the native style (although this was in general deeply disapproved of among the British communities).

In fact, the adult tendency to overclothe children was understandable: houses were largely unheated, medical care had to be paid for, antibiotic drugs did not exist and child mortality was still soaringly high. Wearing warm clothing to avoid catching cold, and the more serious illnesses which might arise from it, seemed merely a sensible precaution.

It is almost impossible to overemphasize the role played by jerseys and other knitted garments in the relaxation, and even democratization, of children's clothes. As a general principle, woollen garments were warm,

'Boys and Girls from a Poorhouse', from an album of life in Ipswich, by Robert Jarrow Jr Photograph, 1855
V&A: PH.152–1979

as Gustav Jaeger and his followers had so passionately argued in the 1880s and 90s. If a child in a poorer family needed a warm garment, the knitted jumper and cardigan were a godsend to any parent who could use knitting needles and either afford new yarn or unravel an old garment to reuse. Patterns were published free in popular periodicals, and easily copied out if a neighbour had one. Illiteracy in the poorer elements of the population has been overstated, taking no account of variations of standard. While few could have read Shakespeare or *War and Peace*, many families had at least one member, and often more, who could read a newspaper, write out a recipe or poem, and make sure that their change was correct when shopping. Even in the 1840s, many of the labouring children interviewed for the *Appendices to reports and evidence submitted to the Children's Employment Commission 1842* could read and write a certain amount.

Photographs of groups of children from Board schools provide some of the best evidence of the increased use of knitting in clothing children: before the 1890s, many of the children are wearing garments – particularly jackets – that are too large or too small, and doubtless in some cases so worn out that they provided little warmth. By the 1910s, many of the children, and certainly the majority of the boys, are wearing knitted garments instead. Knitted clothing also had the advantage of a certain amount of elasticity to accommodate a child's growth, and was thrifty. If need be, a jumper could be unravelled and knitted up again in a larger size, with a contrasting welt and cuffs of some other yarn, or in stripes using up several old garments.

'A Scale of Stockings and
Socks', from *The National
Society's Instructions on
Needlework and Knitting*
Scale table and stitch
guide, with white woollen
knitted stocking sample,
1838
V&A: T.307–1979

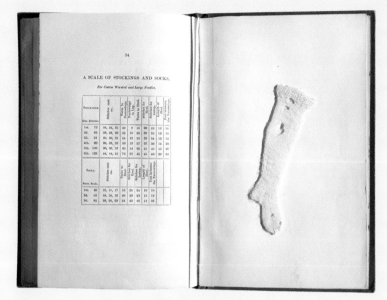

There was still competitiveness in laundering. A child attired in clean
clothes, particularly if they included white garments, continued to
be an indicator of respectability in all but the poorest circles. As a
consequence, children's cotton and linen garments were often starched
and pressed to rigidity, for starching not only presented a smart
appearance, even in old cloth, but repelled a certain amount of dirt.

> Each time you put on a clean chemise the starch in the lace pricked
> like a small frill of thistles round the neck … Getting dressed, as may
> be imagined, was a matter of a good hour's hard work … A minimum
> of forty buttons contributed to the 'decent' turnout of a little girl.
> (M. Steen in *The Years of Grace*, ed. Streatfeild, 1950)

Much of all this changed forever in the aftermath of the First World
War. Nobody seems able to pinpoint the exact causes, but there were so
many changes in the way of life that it is perhaps not surprising that it
affected clothing and childhood too. Children's mourning was among the
customs which died out, as was breeching (although babies continued to
wear dresses, irrespective of gender, until the 1960s).

This period saw nothing less than a revolution in childrenswear, which
had been long enough in coming. The oft-repeated pleas of reformers
such as Cadogan in the 18th century and Ada Ballin in the 19th were
helped by the introduction of more washable, colour-fast, lightweight
fabrics and fabric finishes, and simpler styles of garment. This
eventually gave rise to what might be called classic children's clothes:
garments that emerged during the last decades of the 19th century and
the first decades of the 20th, and have endured almost ever since.

Boys now wore trousers of some sort as soon as they could walk, and
there was considerable emphasis in dressmaking books on producing
their garments with a 'manly' (i.e. plain and tailored) appearance, as
if to put a distance between the modern child and the only recently
discontinued tradition of boys' dresses. This did not, of course, prevent
magazines such as *Good Needlework and Knitting* giving instructions
for a smock to make for a little boy in October 1935: it was in a
masculine shade of blue, for one thing.

Fabric, yarn and clothing manufacturers used the bright but muted
colours then considered most appropriate for children, such as almond
green, lemon, saxe blue and cherry red. Tan or brown were generally
preferred to black, and there was a definite absence of strong colours
such as royal blue, purple and emerald. In August 1927, Selfridges
Bargain Basement stocked a pullover for the two- to six-year-old age
range in 'brick, orange or maroon mixture', but it was an exception.
Even in the bargain ranges, their children's woollens were far more
often made in shades of fawn, grey, blue and pink.

In the 1930s, there was considerable divergence between adults' and
children's clothes. While adults dressed increasingly in formal garments,
dark colours and substantial fabrics, children's clothing changed little
from its late 1920s format. The garments that achieved their classic
status in childrenswear at this time included the kilt, jumper, T-bar
shoe, double-breasted tailored coat and blazer, and for girls, the smocked
dress. The popularity of these garments over a large part of the 20th
century is unsurprising: childrenswear has a history of slow change, and
the 19th century had been distinctly unusual in seeing so many different
styles and changes. Parents liked classic garments because they allowed
for growth, were conservative in taste (removing much of the need to
keep up with fashions) and tended to be well made, all of which made
them easy to use for more than one child.

Smocked dress, from
a Selfridges newspaper
advertisement, 1931
V&A: MoC

Manufacturers benefited in the short to medium term because their ranges did not require such constant design updates, and their products built up customer loyalty through good value. From the child's point of view, it could be argued that the slow changes in fashion removed a good deal of peer group pressure.

In the long term, however, the manufacturers eventually paid the price for the simplicity and stability of these fashions: not only were some of them easily and more cheaply made at home, many of the commercially produced ones were so well made that they effectively never wore out, leading to fewer purchases and lower profits. And there was pressure from the retail trade too. By the late 1930s, it appears that childrenswear buyers in department stores were demanding some degree of exclusivity. The trade press reported that

> Although manufacturers may feel that the volume of business does not justify this action, buyers say that they are forced to do it for their own protection … Manufacturers say that they almost find themselves in the position of private dressmakers, and that if the matter is allowed to go any further they will soon be making only one frock in a particular style. Whilst they wish to co-operate as much as possible, they do feel that some buyers do not appreciate the extra production costs involved.
> (*The Children's Outfitter*, January 1938)

The editorial explanation for this was concern about rival outlets offering the same item at different prices; but apart from the fact that competitive pricing was the normal situation, and always had been, it is quite clear that the area in which the pressure for exclusivity was being brought to bear was specifically that of teen and pre-teen girls' dresses. Perhaps a certain amount of boredom had finally set in.

The Second World War of 1939–45 brought this particular debate to an end. Hostilities – although foreshadowed by the events of the First World War in 1914–18 – impacted on the civilian population as no other conflict had ever done before.

It is true that during the first year of the war, there was little effect on clothing. Photographs of quite lavishly dressed occasions survive. It was, for example, quite usual for a bride to have an elaborate gown and veil, with five or six bridesmaids in matching full-length dresses, all with fashionable trailing bouquets. By the mid-1940s, by contrast, the bride would often be in a suit or uniform, and the bridesmaids wearing what was already in their own wardrobes or could be borrowed from friends or family. This state of affairs persisted in the years immediately after the war.

Brave Girls in War,
front cover from a
propaganda book
published by Raphael
Tuck & Co., early 1940s
V&A: Renier Collection 2A

Almost from the beginning of the war, manufacturers were required to change to the making of munitions and other items required by government, or to give up their buildings and share premises with other manufacturers (the concentration scheme). Shortages of manpower and materials also began to bite. Many of those who worked in industry were called up on active service, and fuel and raw materials were of limited availability.

Purchase Tax was introduced in 1940 in an attempt to reduce the purchase of new items, particularly those which were imported from overseas or were made from imported materials, such as cotton. Imports took up valuable resources such as fuel and manpower, and the ships that brought most of the imports were targeted by enemy bombs. The government needed to make sure that all possible resources went towards the war effort rather than protecting the consumer. This taxation did not achieve the desired result, however, and was demonstrably unfair to poorer customers while making little or no difference to the wealthier ones.

It became obvious that commercially available clothing was one of the categories of item that would need to be tightly controlled by rationing, and the Utility Clothing scheme was introduced in the UK on 1 June 1941, with a distinctive two-crescent logo (nicknamed 'the cheeses') designed by Reginald Shipp.

Utility clothing had to eliminate all unnecessary elements such as trimmings, surplus fabric, double-breasted fastenings and more than a certain number of pockets. The equivalent scheme in the USA, General Limitation Order L-85, was introduced in 1942, but was less rigorous, with exemptions for various categories, including baby and maternity garments. The idea of a non-negotiable form of rationing was not just to limit the number of items available for an individual to buy, but also to guarantee the availability of basic commodities to everyone; although of course it did nothing to address the problem of people being unable to afford the purchase price. Some items, such as hats, were not rationed because it would have been pointless: they were already so scarce that they were difficult to buy, and availability to all could not be guaranteed.

Although there was a distinct shortage of children's clothing throughout the war, not all children's garments that complied with the Utility scheme restrictions were given Utility status automatically. For example, Pasolds Ltd, the original makers of Ladybird clothing, struggled to get their underwear and dressing gowns recognized under the original scheme, despite the garments' eminent suitability and the company's highly efficient production methods and recycling

Clothing coupons from
a ration book, 1940s
V&A: Theatre Museum Archive

programme (one of their main claims was that they produced two
tons of cotton cloth for every ton of cotton yarn allocated to them).
The reason appeared to be that few firms were making them, and
so they were not included. Smocked baby garments over 22 inches
(56 cm) in length fell foul of the 1944 update of the regulations,
because it was thought that smocking the fabric across the chest
would expand a baby's long gown by enough to allow an older child to
wear it somehow (A. Guppy *Children's Clothes 1939–1970*, pp.148–9).

Clothes rationing in the UK was operated by the annual issuing of
coupons to each member of the population: the allowance was 66 in the
first year, but gradually decreased as the war went on, and reached
its lowest level with 36 in 1945. A new garment for sale had not only a
price, but a value in these coupons. There was originally an exemption
for babywear, but this lasted for only a few months, and even terry
towelling nappies were included when baby clothes were added to the
schedule of rationed items. It soon became apparent that the number
of new garments anyone could have in a year was very limited indeed,
and that for anyone other than the youngest children, it was advisable
to save the coupons for items such as coats and shoes that could not
easily be made at home. Such was the difficulty in clothing children
that families sometimes had to use the adults' coupons to get new shoes
or winter coats for children who had outgrown their old ones (although
it was technically illegal to give coupons to someone else). Alice Guppy,
wartime editor of the clothing trade magazine *The Children's Outfitter*,
asserts that it was in fact deliberate government policy to assume
that this would happen (*Children's Clothes 1939–1970*, p.92). Wading
through the mass of regulations and counter-regulations, quotas,
ignorance, rivalry and bureaucracy which Guppy and Eric W. Pasold
(*Ladybird Ladybird*) describe, the wonder of it is that children in the
UK had any clothes at all at this period.

Some compromises were more accepted than others: shoes with
wooden soles (sometimes hinged) to save on leather, for example,
were enthusiastically worn by many, and could apparently still find a
market in the 1950s. But apparently no-one was willing to give up the
distinction between boys' garments which did up left over right, and
girls' which did up right over left, not even for something as otherwise
identical as a school blazer. Two of the shortages most greatly felt in
childrenswear were those of plimsolls and wellington boots, because
of the scarcity of rubber after the loss of the major centre of rubber
tree growing, Singapore, to the Japanese forces early in 1942.

There was also a black market in various rationed goods, including
new clothes. Even more temptingly, clothes coupons were sometimes
traded: those who had money to spare could buy more coupons and

those who were too short of cash to buy new garments could sell an otherwise useless asset. As a way of trading, the black market avoided the rationing regulations, but was breaking the law and was regarded in some quarters as treasonable: '… any man who deliberately evades the law and sets out to make a handsome profit out of that evasion in wartime, is as much a fifth-columnist [supporter of the enemy] as if he were in direct touch with the enemy …', states Captain James, RN, one of the characters in M. Pardoe's children's novel *Bunkle Butts In* (1943).

The only realistic alternative was to buy second-hand garments, swap clothing with other people, or make your own, either from new fabric (which still took coupons, but fewer) or to use old garments to make new ones, encouraged by the Make Do & Mend campaign. This took its name from a Ministry of Information booklet issued in 1943, and featured a character called Mrs Sew-and-Sew. The associated slogan was 'Mend and make-do To save buying new'. The joint emphasis was on taking better care of the clothes that were in use, and using others to make a new garment (making a new dress from two old ones, or mittens from men's socks, for example). There was nothing inherently new in this, of course, but the government had to be seen to encourage thrift and recycling in aid of the war effort, and to give the civilian population information on how best to achieve this. Another of M. Pardoe's fictional characters, Jill de Salis, a schoolgirl in her mid-teens in 1943,

> *was the easiest to provide for, because she was nearly as tall as her mother now, and could often make do with some of Mrs de Salis's old country clothes with only a very little alteration … Bunkle [the youngest], too, could wear a lot of Robin's cast-offs, but Robin always seemed to have to have everything new, and it was a puzzle in wartime to find him what he really needed and to make the coupons go round.*

Jane's party frock
Cotton and silk patchwork
British, 1944
V&A: Misc.265–1983

As so often in the past, the family that had sewing and mending skills was at a great advantage. So too (although government would never have allowed Mrs Sew-and-Sew to admit it) was the better-off family who in pre-war days had had the space and the money to acquire and store unused items, which could now be made into something else. It was hard on poorer families to be told to reuse old sheets or towels for various purposes, for example, when they probably had none to spare.

Of necessity this austere approach to clothing continued in the UK and many other countries after the war, and on into the 1950s. Money and materials were still short, which in turn led to a shortage of stock in the retail trade, and even to continuing shortages for the home dressmaker and knitter. The knitting and sewing skills which had been so important for the clothing of civilians during the war continued to be needed.

Large numbers of children experienced the 1950s as a kind of second-hand version of the 1930s. Industry was recovering, but slowly, and there was little or no money for redevelopment or new design. There was also a psychological need for the familiar and reassuring: no real wonder that many companies returned to producing their pre-war ranges, although some childhood staples, such as matching frocks and knickers, or coats and hats, became hard to find (Selfridges were offering a rare example of Dayella frock and knicker sets for younger girls in 1950, for example), and finally ceased to be made.

The financial and industrial (and therefore consumer) situation was quite different in the USA:

> I can't imagine there has ever been a more gratifying time or place to be alive than America in the 1950s. No country had ever known such prosperity. When the war ended the United States had $26 billion worth of factories that hadn't existed before the war, $140 billion in savings and war bonds just waiting to be spent, no bomb damage and no competition. All that American companies had to do was stop making tanks and battleships and start making Buicks and Frigidaires – and boy did they. (Bill Bryson, *The Life and Times of the Thunderbolt Kid*, 2007)

While innovative teenage fashions were continuing to emerge in large numbers in the USA, in Britain, the Commonwealth and continental Europe, teenagers continued to dress in conservative ways: there was little alternative.

Fashion designer Digby Morton (1906–83) considered the following to be 'must-have' clothes for a British girl entering her teens in 1950:

> A well-tailored long coat in navy, green, dark beige, tan or grey
> A grey flannel suit (jacket and skirt)
> At least two other day skirts to tone with the coat
> A couple of day dresses
> A selection of woollies, cardigans, blouses
> A party frock
> An evening skirt or two with amusing jumper tops
> A finger-tip (length) velveteen swing jacket for evening
> (or a white rabbit fur cape)
> (Noel Streatfeild [ed.], *The Years of Grace*, 1950)

Morton begins by enthusing over the way contemporary clothes for the teenage girl were *not* miniatures of grown-ups' clothes, but goes on to say: 'If I were Prime Minister I would make it compulsory for every girl to have a grey flannel suit'; his suggestions for teenagers' clothes sound remarkably adult, apart from the white rabbit fur cape which to most people at the time would have suggested a much younger wearer. Trousers, arguably the most important garment in the post-war girl's wardrobe, are completely absent from the list.

Retail trade in clothing had improved a good deal by the late 1950s, particularly in the chain stores such as Marks & Spencer, and via the mail-order catalogues, which often stocked slightly different lines, but most children still wore a mixture of shop-bought and home-made clothes, and some still belonged to families who made use of a local dressmaker. Far-reaching changes began in the 1960s, although in childrenswear '60s fashions' didn't get under way on a large scale until 1964–5.

The emergence of strong contemporary design in general, much of it Scandinavian-inspired, with clean and uncluttered shapes and unusual colours, was equally evident in clothing. Mary Quant, Pierre Cardin, Foale and Tuffin, and Yves St Laurent were among the leading designers who went on to produce clothing for children as well as adults. Boutique shopping, and the development of trendy retail outlets such as Biba including children's ranges, all added to a sense of high fashion. Even for a child it could feel like social disaster to appear in old-fashioned clothing, and the shift dresses, flared trousers, long waistcoats, kipper ties and capes, often in bright colours and new synthetic fabrics, could hardly have been more different from the clothes they had been wearing before.

In fact, these were largely child-friendly fashions, and adults could dress as children, too, if they wished. An illustration in the teenage magazine *Petticoat* (18 February 1967) of a young adult modelling a 'little girl' dress and sucking her thumb, was quite acceptable by the standards of the day.

In childrenswear, particularly in occasion wear, two of the many changes that turned long-established thinking on its head were the return of black on the one hand, which has lasted, and the acceptability of a less austere appearance for boys' clothing on the other, which has not. Black, which had been considered by many parents to be totally unsuitable for children for much of the 20th century, especially after the two wars of 1914–18 and 1939–45, was suddenly popular, even for younger children. Colourful prints and shades (notably pink) and the use of lace, were acceptable for boys, although they have since lost ground again to more sober colours and overtly 'masculine' appearance.

At this point, it was wearing the fashionable look that mattered, more than the brand, although naturally a teenage girl who had access to Biba fashions, for example, had an edge over her friends who did not. This statement now sounds impossibly quaint – why would someone not have access to a particular brand of merchandise? – but is an indication of the vast changes in the retail trade over the last forty years. Before the mass development of shopping centres and the availability of online shopping, there were still large groups of the UK populace who had little or no access to some of the most fashionable shops and their products.

This perhaps explains why home dressmaking continued to be important in the 1960s and 1970s. The simpler lines and structures of fashionable garments often made it possible to make acceptable copies of high-street fashions at a fraction of the cost, and extremely quickly. 'My daughter had nothing to wear to a school disco, so I made her a shift dress in an evening' was a not untypical comment.

The Sussex-based firm Clothkits made a considerable contribution to helping the home dressmaker. Founded by Anne and Fin Kennedy in 1969 and lasting until 1988, the firm produced very distinctive and decorative clothes for women and children, mainly in the form of garment pieces printed on fabric, ready for cutting out and sewing. The phenomenon was not new (various degrees of partly made-up garments had been available since the glory days of *Myra's Journal* in the 1880s and 1890s); but what was innovative was the use of pattern and colour, and the fact that if there was any space to spare on the fabric, another small item such as a bag or a doll's dress was often included in the printing.

Harrap Bros
(Sirdar Wools) Ltd
knitting pattern for
boys' helmets, 1939
V&A: Misc.615(33)–1984

Hand knitting, by contrast, was somehow deemed old fashioned (although it did revive in the early 1970s, with the craze for picture sweaters, and has remained popular where dressmaking has not). Hand knitting at this point was associated with the war years of the 1940s, and the austerity of the immediate post-war period. Perhaps this was partly because during the wartime-related shortages, knitting had sometimes been used to create garments for which it was not really appropriate. Knitted woollen swimsuits are an embarrassing childhood memory for many who were born in the 1930s and 1940s: coming out of the water often meant that the costume, having become thoroughly saturated, sagged down the body, baring more than was intended.

Crochet was certainly not regarded in the same way, and indeed had a popular revival, particularly in the making of 'granny squares' which even a beginner could join together to make a simple shoulder bag.

It was also eminently well suited to making many of the fashionable garments of the 1960s and 1970s: shift dresses, ponchos, floppy hats, berets and tank tops.

A counter to the new fashions was what seems to have been the beginning of the modern vintage fashion movement – the craze among young people in their teens and twenties for wearing antique and obsolete clothing, notably Victorian nightgowns and military uniforms. These items were low cost (as antique clothing continues to be, in many cases) and were readily available. In general they were worn deliberately skewed in some sense to signal that 'anything goes' – an army uniform jacket with a pair of ripped jeans and long hair, for example, or a Victorian nightie worn with a red ribbon sash for a party – and the suspicion that the original wearer would have been horrified added to the appeal. The military greatcoat was one of the few garments of this type that was worn in a straightforward way, and was good value in the practical sense.

While younger children did not wear antique garments (which would not in general fit a modern child) their clothes certainly once more showed a historicizing tendency, with the reintroduction of mob caps, pinafores, breeches, lace jabots and long-skirted dresses, particularly for occasion wear.

The 1970s were arguably the last decade with distinctive, encapsulated fashions. The evidence of television repeats such as the later series of *Father Dear Father* demonstrates that the yoked and empire line dresses, loon trousers, tank tops, tiered skirts, shirts with full sleeves and long-pointed collars, and wide flamboyant ties were exaggerated forms of what had originated in the 1960s.

From then on, clothing has become increasingly eclectic, with numerous cultural influences and revivals (sometimes within twenty years: leg warmers, for example) and also the increasing use of vintage garments, even for children. There is a current bout of nostalgia for the more evocative looks in children's clothing of recent years, of which Biba and Clothkits are two of the prime examples, and such garments can regularly be found on eBay.

If fashions become less distinctive, then the garment itself becomes less important, so there is less point in being able to copy it at home. No longer can a magazine say '… why wait for the shops? Sew yourself an original for half the price' (*Petticoat* magazine, 18 February 1967). It is far more acceptable to have bought it, or had it bought for you, and for many children, to have the visible label that proves that it's 'the real thing'. Increasingly, too, people no longer have the necessary sewing skills or the time. In a recent magazine article on Clothkits, the majority of the interviewees felt that they were too busy to find time to spare for making clothes for their children, even with the process partly completed for them.

Biba garment label,
1960s or 1970s
V&A: E.3681–1983

Children on
a street corner,
by John Heywood
Photographic print, 1982
V&A: Misc.1082–1992

Commercially produced garments began to make up the bulk of most
children's wardrobes, and brands became the most important element,
whether a 'cool' label such as Converse, or a budget brand like
Primark. Retail childrenswear has polarized to a large extent,
with the high-profile brands considered of prime importance, to the
extent of their logos and names being pirated. This, together with
the infringement of copyrighted design, is now a major target for
criminal investigation and litigation, in contrast to the past, when
such practices were more widely tolerated and protection was minimal.
Much of the rest of the custom goes to chain stores which have cut-
price designer ranges (such as Debenhams' Jasper Conran range)
and retailers specializing in obviously cut-price clothing that can
readily be discarded. Much agonizing goes on over children wearing
inappropriately adult fashions – and underwear. A bra for a seven- or
eight-year-old may well come to be as accepted as a liberty bodice (once
also a new development) was by 1930.

One of the main innovations of recent years has been the real growth in
character merchandise clothing. The very first character merchandise
for children was probably the stamp folder *The Wonderland Postage
Stamp Case*, devised by Lewis Carroll in the 1890s to accompany the
success of his earlier *Alice* books. Other items derived from films and
books followed, and the name of the child film star Shirley Temple
(born 1928) appeared in the late 1930s on the labels of what was
probably the first range of children's clothing to be linked in this way.
A Shirley Temple dress in the V&A Museum of Childhood collection

Salt, Mustard,
Vinegar, Pepper,
by Alec Brooking
Photographic print,
1975–85
V&A: B.27–1998

was brought back from the USA for a British child by her father, who
was in the clothing trade himself. Well made and simply but elegantly
styled, the blue and white dress is a startling contrast to many of
its more traditional contemporaries, and was clearly worn until it
would fit the child no longer, as the much let-down hem shows. Such
an item would obviously confer real prestige on a child among her
contemporaries, even in a less commercially orientated age.

The Disney Corporation was probably the first to produce character
promotion on a global scale in children's clothing. One of its most
notable successes in everyday clothing has been the cartoon version
of A.A. Milne's *Winnie-the-Pooh*, with licensing arrangements for
manufacturers to make everything from pyjamas to lanyards.

Moreover, in an age when fancy dress is seldom used, and in any
case viewed rather self-consciously, by children as well as adults, the
commercial success (and marketing hype) of fantasy films such as the
Harry Potter series and the *Pirates of the Caribbean* trilogy have given
an unexpected lift to dressing-up clothes and accessories relating to the
main characters.

In considering three centuries of children's clothes, it becomes very
apparent that clothes are important – certainly the right clothes. In the
children's 1920s novel *The Secret of the Dusty House*, by Winifred Pares,
Susan is a penniless orphan who arrives to live with a better-off family,
bringing just one set of shabby clothes and the unenviable status of

charitable dependent. A wealthy relative of theirs sends several boxes of luxurious (and in many cases vulgar) cast-off garments, and Susan starts her rehabilitation when she gains a plain silk-lined tailored tweed suit, left over when all the frilly blouses have been spoken for. 'Is that the tweed from Aunt Lena's treasure boxes? Well it just suits you. And you look so happy. Clothes do make a difference, it's quite true', comments her guardian. The author's not particularly subtle point is that Susan (who of course turns out to be Lady Susan) has instinctively better taste than her guardian's family, some of whose members fall into further vulgarity by (among other things) assuming that they are superior.

The wrong clothes can have an even greater effect and seem to provide far more scope for most writers, whether dealing with fact or fiction. Eleanor Farjeon (born 1881), wrote of her unease as a child at wearing her Swiss dressing-up costume to a party (instead of her usual pink silk party frock), at an adult's request: '... mine was the most noticeable dress. Nobody but I was wearing "fancy dress", and I felt conspicuous and singled out.' The attractive but unusual dress intensified her embarrassment when she made a mess of her 'party piece' recitation:

> If only I had on the Surah Silk! Among all the other little girls in silk and
> lace dresses I might presently have been lost, and my shame forgotten.
> But wherever I went my black-and-scarlet proclaimed me ...' This is
> the little girl who forgot her piece and cried!'
> (E. Farjeon, A Nursery in the Nineties, 1980)

The effect is most obvious in a community like a school, where there are usually unwritten as well as written rules on what is, or is not, acceptable. This seems to be particularly true of boys' schools (male attire post 1800 being particularly conservative). It can be a very effective device for writers of novels set in this environment, and frequently indicative of a good deal about the characters. In *Tom Brown's Schooldays*, Tom arrives at Rugby School wearing a cap rather than a hat: '"Hullo though," says East, pulling up, and taking another look at Tom; "this'll never do. Haven't you got a hat? We never wear caps here. Only the louts wear caps"' (T. Hughes, *Tom Brown's Schooldays*). On the way up to school, East persuades Tom to buy a new hat, 'a regulation cat-skin at seven-and-sixpence', which reinforces the point that Tom is willing to change himself to fit into his new environment. The novel is set in the 1830s – Hughes was at the school from 1834 to 1842, and based the character of Tom on his brother George.

In Anthony Powell's novel *A Question of Upbringing* (volume 1 of *A Dance to the Music of Time*, 1951), the unsuitability of the 'wrong overcoat' once worn by Kenneth Widmerpool at his school (clearly Eton just after the First World War, although not specified as such) is at first sight less clear:

> *My impression is that the overcoat's initial deviation from normal was slight, depending on the existence or absence of a belt at the back, the fact that the cut was single- or double-breasted, or, again, irregularity may have had something to do with the collar; perhaps the cloth, even, was of the wrong colour or texture.*

But as Powell goes on to explain,

> *As a matter of fact the overcoat was only remarkable in itself as a vehicle for the comment it aroused, insomuch that an element in Widmerpool himself had proved indigestible to the community.*

And sure enough, Widmerpool goes on proving 'indigestible' as an adult. We are indeed what we wear, sometimes from an unexpectedly early age.

Wolf Cub enrolment
certificate
Printed card, 1923
V&A: B.34–1993

Boys' Timeline

1700

Basic garment types continue the
traditions of the previous century.
Formal-looking garments
(coat, knee breeches, shirt).
Younger boys wear dresses.
Shirt is the main undergarment for boys.

1725

Few changes to fashions.
Younger boys wear dresses.

1800

Few changes to main fashions.
Novelty hussar fashions
introduced for younger boys.

The Fight Interrupted,
by William Mulready
(detail), 1816
V&A: FA.139[0]

1825

Few changes to main fashions.
Hussar styles and skeleton suits
go out of fashion after *c*.1830.
Younger boys wear dresses; tunics
with trousers introduced in the1840s.
Drawers more generally worn
as part of boys' underwear.

Suit for a boy, 1820–30
V&A: T.144(&A,B)–1962

1900

Few changes to main fashions.
After about 1920, shorts replace
dresses for youngest boys.

Boy at a church clipping
ceremony, from a photograph
by Benjamin Stone, 1902
V&A: E.2330–2000

1925

Emphasis on lightweight but
washable and hard-wearing clothes.
Few changes to main fashions.
Scotch and sailor suits now old-
fashioned except for formal wear.
Second World War brings clothes
rationing and Utility Scheme.
Resumption of 1930s styles
after the War.

Boy Birdnesting, print
by Eric Ravilious, 1927
V&A: E.582–1972

1750

Few changes to fashions.
Younger boys wear dresses.

Boy fishing,
detail of tile, 1758–61
V&A: C.54–1967

1775

New, less formal fashions start to
be worn, but change is gradual.
French Revolution (1789–99)
accelerates change to new fashions
(notably short jacket and long trousers).
Youngest boys still wear dresses,
but from 1790s skeleton suits and
similar garments also popular.

Boy's linen
suit, c.1780
V&A: T.184&A,C–1961

1850

Jackets become longer in length.
Scotch and sailor suits become
popular towards end of period,
as do historicizing fashions such
as the Fauntleroy suit.
Tunics with trousers go out
of fashion by 1860s; short
trousers worn until teens.
Youngest boys wear dresses.

Boy in tunic and trousers
from fashion plate, 1851
V&A: E.513–194

1875

Suits of matching garments
fashionable for all age groups.
Scotch and sailor suits remain popular.
Short trousers worn until teens.
Youngest boys wear dresses.
Introduction of simpler styles advocated
by clothes reformers about 1890.

E. Goodson wearing a three-piece suit,
photograph by J. Cooper of Wigan, 1880–90
V&A: MoC

1950

Few changes in fashion to begin with,
especially for younger boys.
Teenage fashions introduced from
the USA from about 1953.
Introduction of new design-led fashions
such as coloured shirts, flares etc. c.1965.
Popularity of historicizing styles, e.g.
Victorian jackets, lace-trimmed shirts.

1975

Return to plainer fashions
and darker colours.
Importance of designer labels.
Increasing use of
synthetic fabrics.

Primark, boy's shirt
and jeans, 2003
V&A: MoC

2008

Girls' Timeline

1700

Basic garment types continue the traditions of the previous century. Formal-looking garments (full skirted long dresses) for all age groups. Corsets generally worn, with several petticoats.

1725

Few changes to fashions.

Plaque showing two girls, 1750–55
V&A: 414(829)–1885

1800

Continuation of neoclassical styles. Novelty hussar fashions, particularly on coats and spencers. Drawers added to underwear about 1810.

Girl singing, from a cartoon by James Gillray, 1809
V&A: 1232(73)–1882

1825

Continuation of neoclassical styles but with more trimming. Bodices become gradually longer, and corsets in general use again. Elaborate sleeves are a fashionable feature, especially in the 1840s. Crinoline petticoats become popular towards end of the period.

Mary Wright, the Carpenter's Daughter, by William Mulready, c.1828
V&A: FA.162[0]

1900

Continued popularity of yoked dresses. Liberty bodice introduced in 1908 as an alternative to corsets.

Three young girls, photograph by Louis Langfier, c.1895–1900
V&A: MoC

1925

Emphasis on lightweight but washable clothes. Shorter skirts. Second World War brings clothes rationing and Utility Scheme. Resumption of 1930s styles after the War.

Girl skipping, photograph by her father, Harold Edgerton, 1940
V&A: E.570–1997

1750

Few changes to fashions.

Embroidered
silk gown, c.1760
V&A: T.183–1965

1775

Simpler fashions start to be
worn, but change is gradual.
French Revolution (1789–99)
accelerates change to high-
waisted fashions inspired by
classical Greek dress.
Corsets less generally worn.

Girl at the Royal
Academy Exhibition,
1788
V&A: E.3648–1923

1850

Formal styles return, with full
skirts and emphasis on the waist.
Fashion for crinoline
petticoats at its height.
Shorter skirts for
younger girls.

Family portrait (detail)
by H.R. Miller, c.1850
V&A: B.101–1995

1875

Bustles and emphasis on back
of skirts popular in the 1880s.
Introduction of yoked dresses
and other styles advocated by
clothes reformers c.1890.

Lowther Arcade (detail),
book illustration by T. Crane
and E. Houghton, 1883
V&A: 60 V 159

1950

Few changes in fashion to begin with, especially
for younger girls.
Teenage fashions introduced from the USA from c.1953.
Introduction of new design-led fashions such as
mini dress, flares, etc., c.1965. Popularity of
historicizing styles, e.g. pinafores, long skirts.

Harrap Bros (Sirdar) Ltd, crochet
pattern for a mini dress, 1970
V&A: Misc.534(47)–1986

1975

From c.1980, increasingly
eclectic fashions, including
revivals and retro fashions.
Importance of designer labels.
Increasing use of
synthetic fabrics.

Child models in skirts
and tops, 2005

2008

Dictionary
of Children's
Clothes

aA

air-raid suit *see siren suit*

alice band *see hairband*

aesthetic clothing garments worn
by those who subscribed to the aesthetic
movement, which flourished during the 1870s
and '80s, and required the conscious seeking of
beauty in all things. In terms of clothing, this
led to the rejection of many of the fashionable
garments of the era and a preference for
particular historical or traditional forms.
As a child, the writer Sylvia Townsend Warner
(born 1893) wore traditionally smocked dresses
in suitably plain fabrics, made by a local
woman. 'Patterned materials were ruled out by
my mother. How foolish a field labourer would
have looked following the plough in a patterned
smock!' (S.T. Warner, *Scenes of Childhood and
Other Stories*).

Prinz Luitpold von
Bayern, by F. Grainer
Photographic postcard
German, *c.*1914
V&A: B.102–1993

Smocking in girls' dresses remained popular
and also transferred to other garments.
Although some parents did go so far as to dress
boys in the type of costume favoured by Oscar
Wilde, with knee breeches and lace-trimmed
jacket, the prevalent form of aesthetic garment
for children was the smock dress for girls and
younger children.
dates principally 1880s and '90s as a fashion,
but aesthetic clothing for children had a certain
amount in common with the styles successfully
advocated by the contemporary clothes
reformers, and some forms of it survive
to this day, notably the smocked dress.
derivation *aesthetic* from Greek 'things which
may be sensed'.

alignment *see gender indicators*

Smock dress
Embroidered silk
British, 1890–1910
V&A: Misc.718–1992

angel top a short, full, round-necked top, typically gathered into a round neckband or yoke, and usually for wear over tights or trousers; as the angel top was basically a very short baby dress, it is perhaps unsurprising that the term more or less died out in favour of the simpler 'dress'.

dates peak period about 1965 to 1985. 'For the under one years [*sic*] angel tops and white lace tights were practically uniform' (A. Guppy, on the early 1960s, *Children's Clothes 1939–70*). In modern usage 'angel top' generally describes one with an angel-themed decorative design, and is no longer child-specific.

derivation origin obscure, probably perceived as making babies look angelic, although baby angels depicted in art have traditionally worn nothing, symbolic of their innocence and other-worldly status.

Viyella House, angel top
Printed polyester-cotton blend
British, 1975
V&A: Misc.332–1983

anorak a hooded, long-sleeved outdoor jacket of at least showerproof fabric, originally closed at the front. Adopted from traditional Inuit clothing by climbers and skiers, the later versions usually open at the centre front, with a zip-fastening, and are made in a variety of textiles and finishes (e.g. quilted nylon, fur fabric).

dates as Western garment, 1930s (sports use) to present day; particularly popular for children from the 1960s onward.

derivation from Inuit *annuraaq* 'a piece of clothing'.

Marks & Spencer, anorak
Nylon
British, 1980
V&A: Misc.294–1980

apron a protective piece of fabric, originally linen, gathered into a waistband, sometimes with a bib front to cover the chest, and tied over clothes to protect them from dirt and damage. In a childhood context, aprons were usually for girls and small (pre-breeching) boys, but even this age-limited usage by boys died out in favour of the overall or pinafore during the 19th century. As with pinafores, aprons could be purely decorative, particularly when made of embroidered fabrics or elaborately trimmed; there was a fashion for making party dresses with aprons of matching fabric in the 1950s, which combined both aspects.

dates 14th century to present day.

derivation French *naperon*, *napron*, diminutive of *nape*, *nappe* 'tablecloth'; in English changing from 'a napron' to 'an apron'.

armband a band of fabric worn around the upper arm, in children most commonly to indicate mourning (when black) or membership of or association with an organization (e.g. a child who was financially supported by a friendly society or Masonic lodge would sometimes have an armband signifying this).

dates 18th century to present day.

derivation descriptive.

armlet *see sleeve*

Justin Laczkovic
wearing an armband
Sepia albumen print
British, 1881
V&A: B.82(19)–1995

Apron
Holland and cotton
British, *c*.1840
V&A: Misc.9(19)–1977

beanie, **beanie hat** a close-fitting narrow-brimmed pull-on hat, sometimes worn with the front edge turned or pinned back; popular in both knitted or crocheted yarn and woven fabrics. Since the 1990s, the term is mainly in use for a small brimless hat of wool or fleece.
dates early 1940s onward in USA, 1950s onward in Britain.
derivation from *bean*, slang for head.

Beanie hat
Printed cotton
British, 1979
V&A: Misc.542–1985

bearing cloth, **bearing sheet** a large piece of decorative fabric used to wrap around a baby when carried; the forerunner of the carrying cape and the baby shawl, although there is some pictorial evidence to suggest its usage in cylindrical form. *Also called* **palm**
dates medieval to 18th century. The OED has *berynge sheet* 1570; *bearing cloth* 1601.
derivation from the verb *to bear* in the sense of 'to carry'. In an extract from an 1875 volume of *Notes and Queries* quoted by Phillis Cunnington and Catherine Lucas in *Costume for Births, Marriages and Deaths*, *palm* is equated with *pall*, from the Latin *pallium*, a piece of cloth (now more familiar in a funeral context).

Bearing cloth
Quilted satin
British, 18th century
V&A: MoC

bed 1 wadding or blanket used as part of the swaddling of a baby, being both warm and absorbent. **2** in older babies, a layer of linen as part of underclothes.

dates probably from ancient times onward.

derivation from Old English *bed, bedd*, which has several appropriate meanings beside the association with a place to sleep, e.g. 'a base, a thick layer'.

bed scarf *see* **shrug**

bedjacket, **bed-jacket** a short jacket for wearing while sitting up in bed. Like dressing gowns, bedjackets were once considered important for children to wear to avoid catching cold. *See also* **shrug**

dates 1900s onward as childrenswear, most characteristically 1920s–1940s.

derivation descriptive.

bedsock, **bed sock** *see* **sock**

Bedjacket
Crocheted wool with ribbon
French, *c*.1930
V&A: B.114–1993

bell-bottoms, **bell-bottom(ed) trousers** otherwise close-fitting trousers with the leg flaring out from the knee downward; associated with naval uniform and thence with the sailor suit. William Rowe & Co, of Gosport and New Bond Street, explained in their publication on the sailor suit that there were several possible origins for the width of leg, but the 'more logical' was the ease with which it could be rolled up for climbing or for washing down decks; Rowe's even sold, among other accoutrements for the sailor suit, 'uniform canvas leggings' (a kind of ankle cuff) as used by naval ratings when wide trousers would be inconvenient (*The Royal Navy of England and the Story of the Sailor Suit, c*.1900).

dates first recorded in the 1890s; bell-bottoms were also fashion items in the 1960s and '70s.

derivation descriptive, from the bell shape of the lower trouser leg; *bell* itself is possibly from Old English *bellan* 'to roar, make a loud noise'.

belliband, **bellyband** *see* **binder**

Seafaring Men, by Septimus E. Scott, from *The Royal Navy of England and the Story of the Sailor Suit*
Printed paper
British, *c*.1895–1905
V&A: B.143–1995

belt, **waistbelt** a length of fabric or leather to fasten around the body, usually about the otherwise close-fitting waist; also formerly used to support a weapon.

snake belt an adjustable stretch belt, often of striped fabric, with an S-shaped clasp which originally had snake head(s) on the terminals of the clasp and a scale-like finish.

Swiss belt, **Swiss waistband** a belt, usually back-fastening, curving up to a point and down to a point at the centre front.

dates medieval to present day. Snake belts have been particularly popular with children from the 1930s to present day, but snake-belt clasps date back to at least the 16th century.

derivation Old English *belt*.

Belt (snake belt)
Webbing with mild
pressed steel
British, *c*.1925
V&A: Misc.268–1978

beret a round hat, turned under to a smaller round brim, and worn on the top of the head or to one side, traditionally associated with the costume of the Basque area. Often worn as an item of uniform, e.g. by schoolchildren, Scouts, etc.

dates early 19th century onward.

derivation French, related to Latin *birretum* 'cap'.

Bairns-Wear knitting
pattern for berets
Printed paper
British, *c*.1940
V&A: Misc.615(5)–1984

bib a piece of fabric, usually rounded or squared, tied under a baby's chin to protect clothing from dribbling or from spilled food. Historically, many bibs were decorative rather than absorbent, and there was sometimes an additional pad underneath, called a 'dribble catcher'. *See also **feeder***

dates still current. The earliest printed reference to *bib* is 1580, but the item was in use with other names, e.g. *slavering clout* (dribbling cloth or garment), much earlier. The 1494 portrait by the Maître de Moulins of the two-year-old Dauphin Charles Orland of France (Louvre, Paris) shows him wearing a button-on bib to match his dress.

derivation from Latin *bibere* 'to drink'; the OED debates whether this is because it is worn when a child feeds by drinking (whereas a *feeder* is worn by a child who is eating food) or because the bib 'imbibes' moisture.

bicorne, **bicorne hat** a brimless hat with the profile resembling a straight-edged crescent.

dates 1780s–90s, remaining in some ceremonial forms of dress (one of the types which survived in 19th-century boys' outfits inspired by historical styles).

Like *tricorne*, the term was in use after the hats were originally fashionable.

derivation French, literally two-horned or pronged.

biggin *see cap*

Bicorne (pageboy's costume)
Satin and silk with cut
steel beads
British, *c.*1900
V&A: T.13(C)–1968

Happy Days brand
(Herbert Sharp Ltd),
bib with dribble catcher
Cotton and
embroidered lawn
British, 1920–39
V&A: Misc.688(1)–1986

Bottom right
Bib
Crocheted lustre thread
with ribbon and lace
British, 1922–30
V&A: Misc.158(5)–1984

bikini a two-part swimming or beach costume consisting of bra and briefs.

tankini a bikini with a longer top.

date 1947 onward, although similar garments were worn by bath house attendants in ancient times.

derivation named after Bikini Atoll, Australia, where atomic test explosions took place in the 1940s; the bikini was judged to be equally explosive.

Coopers, for Tesco
Stores Ltd, bikini
Nylon
British, 1983
V&A: Misc.445(1,2)–1984

binder, **belliband**, **bellyband**, **roller**, **swathe**, **sw(e)ather** a length of fabric several inches across, wound round a baby's body to cover the navel, sometimes with a coin over the site of the umbilical cord in the belief that this promoted healing. '… about a yard of flannel that was swathed round and round and safety-pinned on …' (M.V. Hughes, *A London Family in the 1890s*). *Myra's Journal of Dress & Fashion* (1 November 1885) suggested that 'The use of the corset may be said to begin in infancy, for the roller or band which envelopes the new-born infant is a support to the tender frame from the first hour of existence'.

dates possibly from ancient times, as part of swaddling; certainly from the 16th century.

derivation from the verbs describing the action to bind, roll, swathe, etc.

Binder
Twilled cotton
British, 1880–1900
V&A: Misc.178-1982

birthday suit a humorous euphemism for nakedness.

dates 18th century onward.

derivation treating the skin as literally the suit (in the sense of a one-piece garment) in which one was born; possibly satirical, as C.W. and P.E. Cunnington's *A Dictionary of English Costume* cites the usage of 'birthday suit' as a piece of 18th-century court dress for wear on a royal birthday.

black pudding *see pudding*

blanket (baby clothes) *see shawl*

blanket pin *see kilt pin*

What Am I?
by Aristophot Co. Ltd
Photographic postcard
Germany, 1900–15
V&A: B.5–1994

blazer a short single- or double-breasted long-sleeved jacket, fairly light in weight, said to have been originally a sports jacket. Particularly associated with boating, it subsequently became a staple garment for children as well as adults, and a core item of school uniform.

dates *c.*1890 to present day.

derivation from original bright (sometimes alleged to be red) colour.

Girl wearing a blazer,
by E. Davey Lavender
Photographic print
British, 1880–89
V&A: MoC

Bloomer a jacket and skirt over loose ankle-length trousers, designed by Elizabeth Smith Miller. While the outfit was not worn by younger girls, evidently some teenage girls did wear it, particularly in the USA where it originated. 'Alec, if it is a Bloomer, I shall protest. I've been expecting it, but I know I cannot bear to see that pretty child sacrificed to your wild ideas of health. Tell me it isn't a Bloomer!' (L.M. Alcott, *Eight Cousins*, 1875).
dates 1850s–1870s.
derivation pioneered by women's rights and temperance campaigner Amelia Jenks Bloomer (1818–94).

bloomers 1 loose-fitting knee-length *drawers*. **2** a shorter and more substantial version of the Bloomer's trousers, worn by girls and women for cycling.
dates 1 1890s–1910s, considered old-fashioned by the 1920s. **2** 1850s–1860s.
derivation originally eponymous, see above.

Bloomers for a girl
Cotton
British, 1870–1900
V&A: B.598–1993

blouse 1 a girl's or woman loose upper garment with the same function as a dress bodice, and in form probably deriving from the separate form of it, but usually not matching the skirt with which it was worn. *Blouse* has sometimes been used to indicate fastening at the back, as opposed to *shirt*, fastening at the front. **2** the top half of a *sailor suit* for both boys and girls, possibly echoing the word's use as a military jacket (e.g. battledress blouse). **3** a girl's short-sleeved lightweight jumper (knitted garments of this type are often mentioned in school stories, e.g. *Ruth of St Ronan's* by Angela Brazil, 1927).
4 blouse-dress a loose-fitting top for boys, worn with a belt; quite distinct from the use of the word blouse to indicate a dress, which was sometimes found in the 1890s and 1910s.
dates 1 & 2 1850s onward. **3** most characteristic of the 1920s and '30s. **4** 1870s.
derivation French, but of otherwise obscure origin (originally a work garment resembling a rural smock).

blouson *see jacket*

blue for a boy *see gender indicators*

Blouse
Embroidered nylon crepe
Hungarian, c.1966
V&A: Misc.494–1985

boater a flat-topped straw hat with a rigid horizontal brim, originally worn for boating, also a fashion item; later in use as an item of school uniform.

dates 19th century to present day.

derivation from the activity for which it was originally worn.

Boater
Straw with ribbon trim
British, 1870–75
V&A: T.164–1930

bobble cap, **bobble hat** a round knitted cap, often with folded-up brim, with bobble or pompon stitched to the crown.

dates 20th century, probably originating in children's clothing.

derivation descriptive of trim; *bobble* is of unknown origin.

bobby pin see *hairgrip*

Bobble cap
Knitted wool, in the colours
of Dress Stewart tartan
Scottish, *c*.1965
V&A: Misc.803(1)–1988

body belt a short wide tube of knitted yarn, formerly worn by babies around the waist and navel, with the function of a **binder**.
dates approximately 1850s–1930s.
derivation descriptive.

boiled shirt *see shirt*

Patons & Baldwins Ltd,
knitting pattern for a body belt
Printed paper
British, *c.*1965
V&A: Misc.616–1992

bolero originally a man's short jacket. In childrenswear, usually **1** a short form of waistcoat. **2** a similar garment but knitted and with (usually short) sleeves.
dates 1 19th century onward. **2** 1950s–60s.
derivation Spanish *bolero.*

bomber jacket *see jacket*

Bolero
Knitted nylon
and angora yarns
British, *c.*1961
V&A: Misc.53–1987

bonnet 1 a cap-shaped outer hat with a face-framing brim, usually fastening with tying strings beneath the chin, considered particularly suitable for babies and young children even when not fashionable for adults and older girls. Some bonnets, e.g. sunbonnets, also had a *curtain*, a long frill to cover the back of the neck. **2** a round brimless hat, by 1700 no longer in use in England, but still in use in Scotland, as in 'Scots (or Scotch) bonnet', the round hat sometimes worn with Highland dress and Scotch suits.
poke bonnet, **poking bonnet** a bonnet with a projecting (poking) brim.
dates the word was in use for various items of headgear from the Middle Ages onward, e.g. the Turkey bonnet, a tapering cylindrical hat worn by both sexes.
derivation Middle English and Old French *bonet*, possibly originally made from a fabric of the same name.

Bonnet (poke bonnet)
Braided straw,
part-lined with net
over satin
British, 1830–40
V&A: T.78-1963

boob tube (US **tube top**) a strapless top, often elasticated or of stretch fabric, sometimes an aspirational garment (originally with a certain amount of shock value) for pre-teen girls wishing to dress in a more adult fashion.
dates originating in the USA in the 1950s; particularly popular from the 1970s onward.
derivation *boob*, slang for breast; possibly related to *bubby*, a 17th- and 18th-century word for nipple.

boot an enclosed form of footwear, usually made of leather or other strong fabric and extending up the ankle, sometimes to the knee or above.

baseball boot a lace-up ankle boot, usually of canvas, with a non-slip sole and reinforced ankle pads.

Chelsea boot a boot with elasticated panels at the sides.

Derby jail boot a type of knitted boot with a leather sole (from the fact that female prisoners at Derby Jail were employed in making them, *The Workwoman's Guide*).

jodhpur boot an ankle boot with a buckle-through strap around the ankle, originally worn for riding by the British in India, and named for the city of Jodhpur (as were *jodhpurs*).

See also **wellington**

dates the word is recorded from about the 13th century, but the item was in use much earlier.

derivation of uncertain origin; Middle English and Old French *bote* and similar words in other European languages.

bootee originally a short boot or enclosed shoe, the word has become associated with knitted footwear for a baby. The bootee resembles a loose-fitting sock, usually with a drawstring at the top or ankle to keep it from falling off.

dates the item has existed from at least 1866, as shown in an illustration in *Punch* (18 August 1866), although Victorian sources of knitting patterns often used the word *boot* (*Myra's Journal*, 1 January 1876).

derivation diminutive of boot.

Top left
Elcho brand,
baseball boots
Canvas with composition
Indian, *c*.1950
V&A: Misc.325&A–1979

Bottom left
Jodhpur boots
Leather
French/Lebanese, 1982
V&A: Misc.699(1–2)–1984

Below
Boots
Leather
British, *c*.1925
V&A: Misc.123(1–2)–1986

Opposite
Bootees
Knitted wool
British, *c*.1916
V&A: Misc.48(31)–1983

bosom friend a covering, often knitted, for the chest in cold weather.

dates about 1800–1850.

derivation play on words, *bosom friend* originally meaning a close or intimate friend.

bowler, **bowler hat** *see hat*

bow tie *see tie*

Marks & Spencer,
boxer shorts
Cotton
British, 1990–95
V&A: B.285–1997

boxer shorts, **boxers** loose-fitting underpants, originally of white cotton. A current variant is close-fitting and made of stretch fabric.

dates 1940s onward.

derivation resembling the shorts worn in the ring by boxers.

Boy Scout uniform *see Appendix 2*

Boys' Brigade uniform *see Appendix 2*

boys' dresses *see dress*

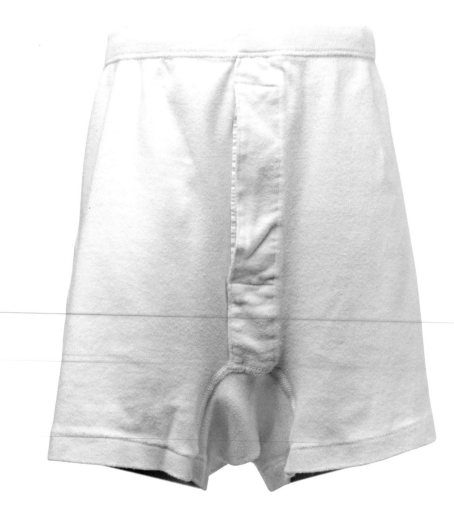

bra, **brassière** an undergarment, usually a construction of two linked cups of fabric, to support the breasts.

bandeau a bra in the form of a piece of fabric wrapped around the breasts.

bra-slip a combination of bra and slip (petticoat).

Teenform™ a brand-name bra made by Berlei specifically for young bra-wearers.

training bra a soft first bra for young girls.

dates early 1900s onward. Elizabeth Ewing in *Dress and Undress* cites an American advertisement of 1907.

derivation this use of the word is unclear. *Brassière* is French, with a number of meanings such as bodice, bib, leading strings, although the French word for bra is *soutien-gorge*. Possibly there was a perceived link with *brace*.

Pasolds Ltd, Ladybird
catalogue entry for bra
Printed paper
British, 1976
V&A: MoC

brace 1 (US and formerly British *suspender*) one of a pair of straps, worn one over each shoulder, to hold trousers, shorts or a skirt in position (the practice of crossing them at the back for a firmer fit was already established by the 1820s at the latest). In 1800 Scrope Berdmore Davies, aged seventeen and in the sixth form at Eton College, bought a 'Pair of Best Silk Elastic Braces with Morocco [leather] Straps' for seven shillings (which was rather more expensive than it sounds, probably about eight pounds in modern money).
2 a partial chest and back cover, sometimes called a **dickey** (a reflection of the word's earlier use to mean a detached shirt front).

dates 1 first in use in the 1780s and still current. **2** unknown, but probably 19th century.

derivation 1 probably from the sense of the word meaning to pull tight or firm. **2** possibly short for embrace (in both cases from Latin *brachia* 'arms', via Old French *brace, brache*).

brace kilt *see kilt*

Brace
Knitted wool
British, 1920–29
V&A: Misc.677–1991

Utility Scheme, braces
Leather and elastic
British, 1942–9
V&A: B.306–1997

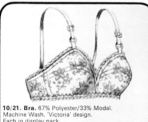

10/21. **Bra.** 67% Polyester/33% Modal.
Machine Wash. 'Victoria' design.
Each in display pack.
Colour: 3/12 solid, Pink **45**, Green **60**.
Approx. Bust: 74cm 79cm 81cm
Code: **10**   **12**   **13**

breeches, **knee breeches** (*also, following older pronunciation,* **britches**) short close-fitting trousers to just below the knee, fastening at the front with a plain vertical button-through opening (a cod placket). From the 1760s they were more likely to have a *fall front* fastening. Even with the introduction of trousers as a fashion in the late 18th century, breeches remained the correct form of dress for formal and evening wear for some years, and also in some institutions. *See also* **buckskins**, **pantaloons**

dates late 16th century onward.
derivation Old English *bréc*.

breeching the now obsolete custom of giving a small boy his first pair of breeches or trousers, usually at about the age of five or six, although this varied considerably from one family to another and at different periods of history. The custom was sometimes accompanied by a celebration, and might also include a first haircut in periods where long hair was associated with younger boys (e.g. 1850–1920) and in wealthier families a first sword (up to about 1800).

dates probably 16th century to about 1920.
derivation from *breeches*, as above.

Breeches
Silk and cotton blend
British, *c.*1760
V&A: T.113(C)–1953

Breeching of Jack Crocker (shown with his twin sister on their third birthday)
Photographic print
British, 1917
Misc.451(1–2)–1991

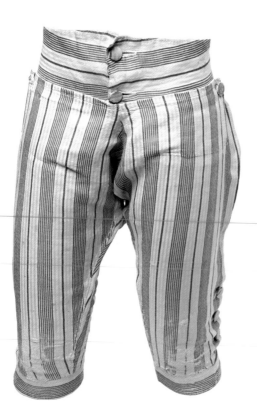

bretelle, **brettle** (in pairs on a dress bodice) either an over-the-shoulder frill, or a vertical panel or strap, sometimes in a contrasting colour. '"She hasn't got any bwetelles [*sic*] to her dwess, and I have," said Maud, settling her ruffled bands over her shoulders, which looked like cherry-coloured wings on a stout little cherub' (L.M. Alcott, *An Old-Fashioned Girl*, 1870).
dates 1850s onward; the form outlasted the name, being still in use on younger girls' dresses in the 1980s.
derivation French for strap or brace.

Laura Ashley,
dress with bretelles
Printed cotton
British/Irish, 1983
V&A: Misc.83–1983

breton, **breton hat** a hat, often of straw, with a domed crown and a broad circular brim up-turned all round, often with a ribbon around the crown and two pendant ribbon streamers at the back. It has been a style much favoured for children's hats, although what appear to be breton hats worn with sailor suits are often flat-crowned hats of naval style: the 'Regulation Senet hat … as worn by bluejackets [naval ratings] on ceremonial occasions throughout the year' (Rowe, *The Royal Navy of England and the Story of the Sailor Suit*, *c*.1900).
dates 1850s–1960s.
derivation from the folk costume of Brittany, France.

Breton hat
Plaited straw
British, 1960–70
V&A: B.910–1993

bridesmaid dress, bridesmaid's dress

as with bridal clothes, a convention has arisen for bridesmaids to wear dresses of a more or less specific type, often with limited connection to current fashions, frequently matching or toning with each other or echoing an element of the bride's dress. Although these dresses were often expected to be worn subsequently as party dresses, in reality this could be quite difficult. 'An unremarkable creation of blue net over blue taffeta, tied at the waist with blue satin and garnished with puff sleeves, net pockets, and rosebuds round the neck and hem, a tradition had grown up concerning its utter ghastliness and complete unwearability' (Antonia Forest, *Peter's Room*, 1961).

flower girl's dress a bridesmaid's outfit, usually for a younger girl who carries a basket of flowers or petals which she strews on the ground in front of the bride.

dates a relatively modern notion, accompanying the establishment of the tradition of the white wedding dress in the 19th century.

derivation descriptive.

briefs *see knickers*

Bridesmaid's dress with cape
Plush
British, 1932
V&A: T.464&B–1976

brogue, **brogue shoe** a type of strong lace-up shoe with bands of decorative patterns punched in the upper.

dates 1900s onward.

derivation Gaelic *bróg* 'shoe'.

bronze shoe, **bronze boot**, **bronze sandal** an item of footwear of 'bronze' coloured leather (in reality a deep and metallic shade of brown).

dates fashionable on and off from the 1860s to the 1930s.

derivation descriptive of supposed colour.

Brownie uniform see *Appendix 2*

buckskins, **buckskin breeches** breeches made from the skin of a deer (buck), or sometimes from sheepskin. Buckskins were hardwearing and considered particularly suitable for boys to wear in the country and for riding and hunting.

dates buckskins were originally gloves or possibly boots of this material, but the term was particularly associated with breeches between about 1770 and 1840.

derivation Old English *buc* 'male deer'.

bunny top see *sock*

Norvic Kiltie brand, brogues
Leather
British, 1930–39
V&A: Misc.262&A–1979

Clarks Ltd, bronze shoes
Leather with pompon trim
British, 1935–55
V&A: Misc.739(1,2)–1992

bunting, **baby bunting**, *also* **baby bag**
a combination of dressing gown and sleeping
bag, often hooded, to keep a baby warm enough
with a minimum of garments or bedclothes;
possibly the precursor of modern swaddling.
dates 1940s onward (*Nursery World*,
20 January 1949).
derivation uncertain, perhaps by association with
the nursery rhyme *Bye, Baby Bunting* ('Gone
to fetch a rabbit skin to wrap the baby bunting
in'). The OED suggests that *bunting* in its sense
of an endearment (first printed mention 1665)
comes possibly from *buntin* 'plump'.

burnous, **burnoose** a flared cloak or
cape, usually with a pointed tasselled hood,
derived from the Arab garment of the same
name, worn by girls and women in the West.
dates 1850s–70s. 'Rose was quite ready to go,
being anxious to try a certain soft burnous
from the box, which not only possessed a most
engaging little hood, but had funny tassels
bobbing in all directions' (L.M. Alcott,
Eight Cousins).
derivation French *burnous*, from Arabic *burnus*.

Joyville brand, bunting
Wool
British, 1980
V&A: Misc.312–1983

Burnoose
Embroidered wool
Indian/British, 1860–69
V&A: Misc.570–1984

busk a narrow length of material such as wood, whalebone or steel, introduced into stays or a bodice for extra rigidity. The word was sometimes applied to a corset in its entirety. Medical practitioners tended to deplore the use of any such aids to rigidity in children's clothing: 'Mr Collier, surgeon of Towcester, gave me a paper on the health of lace-makers … he also told me that much injury ensues to young girls from a habit they have of wearing a strong wooden busk in their stays to support them when stooping over their lace pillows; this being worn when young and the bones soft acts very injuriously on the sternum and ribs' (Major J.G. Burns, from *Appendices to reports and evidence submitted to the Children's Employment Commission 1842*).

dates 16th century to 19th century.

derivation of uncertain origin, possibly derived from Latin *boscum* 'wood'.

Busk in the
waistband of a dress
(viewed from inside)
Metal
British, 1855
V&A: T.403–1971

buster suit 1 a two-part romper consisting of close-fitting top and shorts or knickers, usually buttoning together, for babies of either gender. **2** a shirt and shorts set, usually in matching or toning fabrics, for slightly older boys.

dates most typical of the 1920s and '30s.

derivation probably from the Buster Brown suit, although ironically this was a hip-length tunic over shorts, as worn by the popular cartoon character Buster Brown, created by Richard Felton Outcault and first appearing in the *New York Herald* in 1902. Buster suits in Britain preserved the idea of a two-garment outfit, but the top was either buttoned to, or tucked into, the shorts.

Selfridges advertisement
for a buster suit
Printed paper
British, 1932
V&A: MoC

Babies' HOLIDAY CLOTHES!
LITTLE BOYS'
BUSTER SUITS
Just The Thing—Pretty and Hardwearing

9 DE 548. In good quality casement, which is fast washing colour. The little Blouse has a turndown collar, fastens down the front, and long inset sleeves. The knickers button on to the blouse, and are supported with two shoulder straps. Can be obtained in good shades of Saxe, Green, or Brown. All have buff-coloured Blouses, which are piped to tone with the knickers. In sizes to fit two to four years of age; lengths 18, 20, and 22 inches. PRICE for complete suit

2/11

Postage 2d. extra on 1 suit.
Postage 3d. extra on 2 suits.
(*Bargain Basement, Aisle 17B*)

bustle a pad or frame worn beneath a dress skirt, positioned over the posterior. As with crinolines, those worn by girls were of fairly modest dimensions. Although there is little or no evidence in the form of surviving examples used by the young, it is quite obvious from the construction of some surviving outer garments for girls that a form of support was needed for the skirt back, if only a small cushion attached to tapes. In some cases, particularly for younger girls, it appears from dressmaking magazines such as *Myra's Journal* that the effect was often partly or wholly achieved by attaching a large folded and puffed bow just below the waist back. *Also called* **dress improver**

Fashion plate, dress worn with a bustle
Hand-coloured engraving on paper
French, 1884–90
V&A: E.1283–1959

dates in girls' clothing, particularly associated with the period *c*.1884–90.

derivation possibly from the verb *to bustle*, which is of uncertain origin (perhaps onomatopoeic, from the noise associated with vigorous action).

buttoning *see gender indicators*

carrying cape a layered form of cloak, or coat with cape, worn by babies. Wilena Hitching in her book *Baby Clothing* (1914) shows a shawl converted into a carrying cape by threading ribbon across the width about a quarter of the way down, and folding to form a two-layered effect before gathering at the neck.
dates 19th century – though cloaks were in use in the 1740s (Foundling Hospital list of clothes issued 1742).
derivation descriptive (worn by a baby when carried out of doors). Carrying a child in the arms was the usual practice before the widespread availability of the baby carriage, which did not happen until the 1860s.

cassock a long, coat-like garment, originally of military origin, subsequently an ecclesiastical garment, worn for example by singers in church choirs (most commonly in red, blue or black fabric). In church services and ceremonies, usually worn with a *surplice*.
dates (ecclesiastical) 17th century onward.
derivation of disputed origin, possibly from French *Cosaque* 'Cossack'.

catsuit *see jumpsuit*

caul *see cap*

Carrying cape
Embroidered twill
British, *c.*1887
V&A: Misc.219–1979

charity uniform the earliest form of school uniform was worn by the pupils of schools run by charitable foundations. These charity school uniforms comprised the child's entire outfit, were supplied by the charity in question, and often remained unchanged in style from those worn at the time of the school's founding (in many cases the 17th or early 18th century). The giving of standard clothing ensured that every child had an adequate number of garments, and also reminded them of their dependence upon the generosity of the charity's founders. Such uniforms could also be used in a disciplinary context: a garment would be removed from a pupil's dress as a punishment, giving the offender a conspicuous appearance. They were generally devised to encourage a humble and grateful attitude in the wearer.
dates the earliest English charitable school, the King's School at Canterbury, was founded in about 598, but the majority date from the Middle Ages or later, and have uniform which is 18th-century in format.
derivation descriptive, from Latin *caritas* 'charity'.

cheat a *waistcoat* with a back of a lesser, usually cheaper fabric, or any other garment where cheaper fabric is used for the parts not visible in normal wear, such as wristbands and sleeves.
dates this usage is at least as old as the late 17th century, and was still in use in a Selfridges advertisement for Christmas 1950.
derivation Middle English *chete*, ultimately from Old French *eschaeter*.

Chelsea boot *see boot*

St Marylebone Charity
School uniform on a doll
Wool blend and linen
British (German doll), 1860
V&A: T.181–1959

'Cheat' blouse
Cotton and silk
British, *c.*1915
V&A: B.207–1996

chemise a loose undergarment like a long vest, worn next to the skin. *Also colloquially called* **shimmy**

dates late 18th century to early 20th century; earlier versions were the **smock** and the **shift**.

derivation French *chemise* 'shirt'.

chemisette a chest cover for wear with a low-necked dress. The **habit shirt** (*see* **shirt**) was also sometimes called a chemisette.

dates approximately 1800–1900.

derivation diminutive of *chemise*, as above.

chinos *see* **trousers**

Chemise
Cotton
British, *c.*1840
V&A: Misc.9(3)–1977

choker a close-fitting ornamental band worn around the neck. A simple band of ribbon or fabric was the form most often worn by girls.

dates a fashion associated with Princess Alexandra, who married the Prince of Wales in 1863; revived in the 1960s.

derivation descriptive or humorous (a choker may become tighter with wear, as the throat muscles relax); the verb *to choke* is of uncertain origin.

Choker
Suede and metal
British, *c.*1970
V&A: Misc.161–1985

chrisom a white linen garment or cloths of unknown shape, in pre-Reformation Britain used to cover the sign of the cross made in consecrated oil on a baby's forehead and chest during Baptism, and thus also any child wearing a chrisom. A child who died before the 'churching' (ritual purification) of its mother four weeks after its birth would be buried still wearing its chrisom. Where the child survived, the chrisom was removed and often given to the officiating priest during the churching.

dates medieval to Reformation as a garment; after this the term came to mean any very young baby, whether christened or not. The register of St Denis Backchurch in the City of London records the burial in 1572 of Jane Dykyns and 'a Cresome child of hers unchristened'.

derivation from *chrism,* the consecrated oil used to make the sign of the cross on the child during Baptism.

christening gown, **christening clothes**, **christening robes** garments, often white or cream, worn by a baby for the ceremony of Baptism. During the 18th and 19th centuries there was a popular custom of making christening clothes from the mother's wedding dress. 'The white "Paduasoy" [a type of silk] figured again in the letters … In one, it was being made into a christening cloak for the baby' (Mrs Gaskell, *Cranford*. The incident referred to takes place in about 1780).

dates garments associated with the christening of infants have been recorded since medieval times, but were only worn for the ceremony after the practice of total immersion was discontinued in the 17th century.

derivation descriptive.

Christening bonnet
Crêpe and swansdown
British, 1923
V&A: Misc. 75(2)–1976

Christening gown
and petticoat
Net over silk
British, 1923
V&A: Misc.75(3–4)–1976

Christening robe
Embroidered satin
British, 18th century
V&A: MoC

Circumcision gown, Circumcision clothes

garment(s) worn by infant Jewish boys during the Circumcision ceremony. In more Orthodox families, the garments featured Jewish forms and symbols, but for others, the garments were the long white and cream clothes which were formal baby wear in most Western communities.

dates traditional (Orthodox use).

derivation descriptive.

clip-on hat *see baboushka*

Circumcision gown
Linen with embroidered
insertions
British, 1870–79
V&A: Misc.561–1985

cloak

1 a long bell-shaped outer garment fastening round the neck, precursor of the coat. *Also called **mantle** **2** in baby clothes, see **carrying cape***

gipsy cloak a circular cape with an attached hood to match, mainly in use in the 1870s. 'Little Girl's Gipsey [*sic*] Cloak' listed among children's dress patterns available from *Myra's Dress & Pattern Depot* in December 1879 (advertisement, *Myra's Journal*, 1 December 1879).

dates 13th century onward, although for children it was largely superseded for general purposes by the various forms of overcoat during the 19th century. It continued in use as party wear, mainly for girls, and received an unexpected but short-lived boost in the late 1930s (in 1938 Debenham and Freebody offered an evening cape for girls at 5½ guineas [£5.25] in wine, black or fuchsia velvet; the design, with a high-standing collar, echoing the cloak worn by Snow White in the Disney cartoon of the same name, released in December 1937).

derivation Old French *cloke*, variant of *cloche*, from medieval Latin *cloc(c)a* 'bell', from the shape of the garment.

Cloak
Silk and satin
British, 1830–39
V&A: B.448–1994

cloche, **cloche hat** a close-fitting bell-shaped hat for women and girls.

dates particularly characteristic of the 1920s and early 1930s, when even baby-sized versions were available. There had been close-fitting hats for girls before, notably in the 1880s, but the prevalent shapes had been either the bonnet or various forms of wide-brimmed hat.

derivation French *cloche* 'bell'.

Top
Cloche hat
Felt with petersham
ribbon
British, *c.*1925
V&A: Misc.436–1980

Bottom
Cloche hat, baby version
Crocheted wool
British, 1928–9
V&A: Misc.728–1992

clock the vertical decorative area along the ankle of a stocking.

dates 16th century to 19th century.

derivation uncertain. The OED cites a conjecture that the patterns were of bell-shaped motifs (and so from *cloche*, as above). C.W. and P.E. Cunnington, *A Dictionary of English Costume 900–1900*, suggest that it was originally a gore or insertion in a variety of garments, from that to the stitchery covering its edges, and finally to the decoration only.

Right
Stockings with clocks
Silk and flannel
British, *c.*1880
V&A: Misc.63–1980

clog originally, like the **patten**, a protective type of footwear, usually with a wooden sole. Traditional British workers' clogs were neither of this kind nor the sabot type found often in continental Europe, but were often made of *kip*, a reversed waxed leather, and took the form of an enclosed shoe fastening with a metal clasp. Different shaped toes were said to indicate different work. The clasp fastenings, which were not normally made by the clogmaker, sometimes carried a letter of the alphabet to indicate size, so that they could be matched with the correct size of clog. Later versions for children included a more open style of shoe with a strap fastening.

dates traditional wear, particularly fashionable from the 1970s onward.

derivation origin obscure, probably from another meaning of the word, a thick piece of wood, referring to the wooden sole.

Clog, strap style
Leather and wood
British, 1896
V&A: Misc.116&A-1923

coat a front-fastening long-sleeved garment for outdoor wear. In the 19th and early 20th centuries, coats were sometimes referred to by the French term *manteau* or the anglicized *mantle*. *Also called* **greatcoat**, **overcoat**, **surtout**

frock, subsequently **frock coat** a slim-fitting waisted coat for men or boys.

jigger coat, **swagger coat**, **swing coat** (1930s onward) short, flared coat for women or girls, popular from the 1930s onward; the names possibly derived from the movement of the garment or the gait of the wearer.

dates in the modern sense, 1650s onward.

derivation originally a medieval tunic-like garment, Middle English, from Old French *cote*, of uncertain origin.

Rowe, coat
Tweed
British, 1930–39
V&A: B.1211(1)–1993

cockade a cap or hat trimming in the form of a rosette or similar decoration, usually made of ribbon. When worn by babies and young children, it could be indicative of gender. The convention varied, perhaps the most firmly established in Britain being to associate the true right side of the head with boys, and the true left with girls. *See also **gender indicators*** **dates** 17th century onward.
derivation perhaps from *cock*, because of the comb on the bird's head.

coif *see cap*

Left
Coat in the Arts and
Crafts style
Embroidered silk
British, 1880–95
V&A: B.17–1998

collar a shaped piece or pieces of fabric worn round the neck to finish, decorate or extend the neck of a garment such as a shirt, dress, coat or jacket. The collar could also perform the function of keeping the neck of a garment clean, and on indoor clothing was often detachable for washing, both for boys (e.g. the ***Eton collar***) and girls (e.g. on 1930s–50s dresses). In July 1933 the dressmaking magazine *Weldon's Bazaar of Children's Fashions* had an offer of an embroidered collar and cuffs set for younger girls for one shilling post free, adding, 'they brighten up a frock wonderfully ... and what is still more pleasing from mother's point of view, they will wash beautifully too'.
falling collar a deep collar, often trimmed with lace or embroidery, characteristically found on coats and historicizing costume such as Vandyke dress or Fauntleroy suits.
Peter Pan collar a turn-down collar with rounded points, particularly associated with childrenswear in the 20th century after J.M. Barrie's *Peter Pan*, first staged in 1904.
dates: 1300 onward; still in use as detachable at least as late as the late 1960s. Coats' *Learn to Crochet* booklet (1967) gives instructions for one.
derivation from French *col* 'neck'.

colour *see **gender indicators***

combat or **kombat trousers**
*see **trousers***

Above
Cockade on cap
Ribbon
British, 1875–99
V&A: Misc.358–1979

Right
Collar
Plastic
Italian, 1960–80
V&A: Misc.288(1)–1982

combinations, informally combies

(US **union suit**) a one-piece undergarment with sleeves and legs, replacing separate vest and drawers.

dates at least 1880s to 1930s.

derivation from the *combination* or *union* of two garments (vest and drawers).

comforter *see scarf*

comfi suit *see snow suit*

Combinations
Knitted cotton fabric
British, 1900–39
V&A: Misc.1054–1991

Confirmation outfit, First Communion outfit

usually white or predominantly white garments worn for such ceremonies, sometimes (in France, for example) based on a simplified version of the clothing of religious orders.

dates approximately 1800 onward, probably popularized by the fifteen-year-old Princess (later Queen) Victoria who wore a white outfit for her Confirmation in 1834.

derivation descriptive, from the respective religious services.

convoy coat *see duffel coat*

Natalie Edith Jamison
in a Confirmation or
First Communion outfit
Photographic postcard
British, 1919
V&A: Misc.354–1992

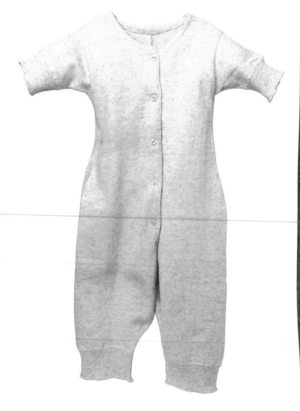

cords, **corduroys** trousers made of corduroy fabric, a ridged cotton fabric with a pile like velvet.

dates men's and boys' working clothes from 1780s onward, becoming leisure and fashion wear in the 20th century.

derivation uncertain origin, popularly said to come from French *corde du roi* 'the king's cord' which in fact does not exist in French; possibly from the surname Corderoy.

Marks and Spencer Ltd,
corduroy trousers
Cotton
British, *c.*1980
V&A: Misc.295–1980

Corset
Cotton stiffened
with cord
British, *c.*1840
V&A: Misc.9(2)–1977

corset(**s**) a restrictive underbodice worn to give a defined shape, particularly to the waist. They were so universally worn, and so widely accepted as being beneficial for all ages, that even physicians had to struggle to persuade wearers that they were harmful and should be given up. Pye Henry Chavasse's response to the question 'When should a girl begin to wear stays?' was an unequivocal 'She ought never to wear them' (*Advice to a Mother*, 1870), and yet they were considered so essential that they were even worn for sports; from the 1880s the less restrictive knitted corsets began to be recommended for athletic and other activities, but Gwen Raverat (born 1885) recalled that as a sixteen-year-old at boarding school, 'We played [hockey] in white blouses and blue skirts, which had to clear the ground by six inches; and our waist-belts were very neat and trim over our tight stays' (*Period Piece*, 1954). In the 1880s and 1890s some manufacturers attempted to produce less restrictive versions for children, such as the 'Ycando Good Sense' corded corsets made by Young, Carter & Overall (*Myra's Journal*, 1 February 1890), which were the forerunners of the *liberty bodice*. Also called **stay**(**s**)

foundation garment usually a 20th-century euphemism for corsetry. 'Sheathalo Mesh Foundation Garments for Girls – a complete corselette in action!' (advertisement in *The Children's Outfitter*, January 1938).

roll-on an elasticated corset applied by standing inside it, pulling it up and rolling it on to the body; introduced in the 1940s.

dates the concept of a tightly-laced waist goes back to ancient times in some civilizations. Corsetry is still in use, although not normally for children. The word *stay* was in printed use from the early 16th century onward, whereas the term *corset* was not introduced until the 1790s.

derivation French *corset*, from Old French *cors* 'body'; *stay* probably from the Old French *estayer* 'to prop'.

costume see *suit*

cravat a wide cloth worn round the neck. The cravat was a precursor of the *tie*, but the two forms were in simultaneous use during the early 19th century. Later used to describe a type of short scarf. *The Winter Book for Girls* (1956) gives a pattern for 'A Crocheted Cravat' for wear over a jumper.

dates 1660s–1840s for boys; by 1850 the tie had become standard wear.

derivation French *cravate* 'Croat' from the scarves worn by Croatian soldiers.

crawlers, creeping overalls *see rompers*

Crinoline
Steel and cotton tape
British, 1860–69
V&A: B.18–2002

crinoline a stiffened petticoat, later a petticoat-shaped frame, to wear under a skirt to make it look fuller. Those worn by younger girls were usually shorter and fuller, to match their short skirts; teenage girls' crinolines were longer and usually narrower. 'I once asked Aunt Etty [born 1843] what it had been like to wear a crinoline. "Oh, it was delightful," she said. "I've never been so comfortable since they went out. It kept your petticoats away from your legs, and made walking so light and easy"' (G. Raverat, *Period Piece,* 1954). In the full-length version the wider skirts could also make the waist appear smaller, and because they swung to the wearer's movement, give an impression of a graceful way of walking.

dates 1840s–60s.

derivation originally made using a mixture of *crin* (horsehair) and wool.

Croc™ a brand of non-slip footwear, originally for outdoor and boating use, but subsequently for fashion and leisure wear. The range includes a number of different styles, but the best-known is a clog with a perforated vamp.
dates 1990s onward.
derivation brand name.

Crocs™
Plastic
Canadian/Italian, 2007
V&A: MoC

cromwell a high-tongued shoe with a large central buckle (often over an instep strap, which was the real fastening), based on 17th-century styles and often worn by children as a formal shoe for parties or weddings. They were typically made of black or 'bronze' leather, but were also available in white.
dates originally 1860s, but particularly popular for children between 1900 and the 1930s; still in use in the 1950s.
derivation adapted from the type of shoe worn by Oliver Cromwell (1599–1658).

Cromwell
Patent leather and mild pressed steel
British, 1953–5
V&A: Misc.63(1,2)–1982

crosscloth a triangular piece of fabric that literally crosses over the head or forehead, worn tied over the forehead beneath a cap or caps (included as part of the swaddling clothes layette).

double crosscloth is also found, probably a square folded into two triangular layers.

Also called **forehead cloth**

dates late 16th century to late 18th century.

derivation descriptive.

Cub, Wolf Cub, Cub Scout uniform

*see **Appendix 2***

cuff a shaped piece of fabric worn round the wrist to finish, decorate or extend the sleeve of a garment such as a shirt, dress, coat or jacket. Cuffs were also used to keep the wrists of garments clean, and were often detachable for washing.

dates 15th century onward.

derivation of unclear origin.

culotte(s) as an item of women's and girls' dress (the usual sense in which the word is used in English) a short divided skirt, usually cut to a flared shape. *Also called* **divided skirt**

dates approximately 1900 onward as a term, 'divided skirt' is the slightly earlier term; in the 1960s and '70s, also worn as a culotte dress.

derivation French *culotte* 'breeches'.

curtain *see **bonnet***

McCall Co. Inc,
sewing pattern
for culottes
Printed paper
USA, 1976
V&A: Misc.347(3)–1983

GIRLS' CULOTTES WITH DETACHABLE BIB AND BLOUSE

PATTERN/PATRON

dD

Danish trousers *see knickerbockers*

Davy Crockett hat, Davy Crockett shirt a hat based on Crockett's raccoon-skin cap; a shirt with a buckskin (or imitation buckskin) strip of fringe across the chest and often the back.

dates popular in the mid-1950s.

derivation Davy Crockett (1786–1836), frontiersman, soldier, congressman, notably as played by Fess Parker in the 1950s film and TV series.

Little Togs brand,
Davy Crockett shirt
Printed twill and
imitation suede
USA, 1955–60
V&A: Misc.547–1986

deely bobbers, deely boppers a narrow plastic headband with a pair of spring-mounted decorations such as stars, feathers or baubles; originally children's novelty headgear patented in the USA in 1982 but sometimes worn by adults. Not to be confused with Deelie Bobbers, a construction toy. *Also called* **feely boppers, disco headband**

dates 1980s onward.

derivation patented by Ace Novelty Co. Inc., USA.

deerstalker a type of close-fitting cap with earflaps, originally of cloth but later versions for children were more often knitted. A deerstalker could also be worn with the flaps up, usually fastened together at the crown. *Also called* **ear cap**

dates 1880s–1950s. Bestway and Patons were among those producing knitting patterns for children's deerstalkers in the 1950s.

derivation originally worn by deer hunters.

denims *see jeans*

Below
Deely boppers
Plastic with metal
Taiwanese, 1982
V&A: Misc.44–1983

Opposite
Bestway knitting pattern
for a deerstalker
Printed paper
British, 1950–53
V&A: Misc.323(3)–1987

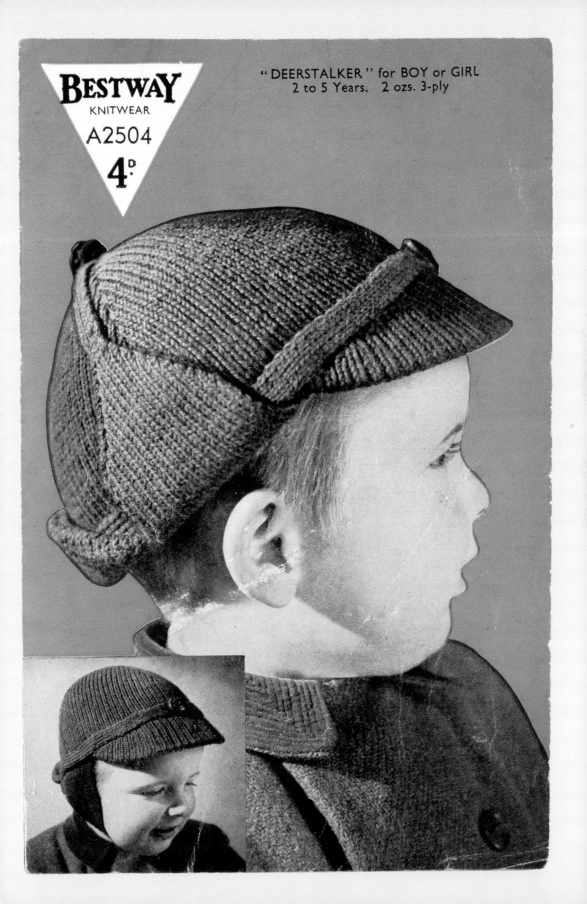

"DEERSTALKER" for BOY or GIRL
2 to 5 Years.   2 ozs. 3-ply

derby a type of lace-up shoe with the paired tabs for the lace holes positioned on top of the body of the shoe; in children's shoes generally more widely found than *oxfords*.
dates 1870s onward.
derivation the English town of the same name.

derby hat *see hat*

Derby jail boot *see boot*

diaper *see nappy*

dickey *see brace*

dinner jacket *see evening dress*

directoire knickers *see knickers*

disco headband *see deely bobbers*

divided skirt *see culotte(s)*

drainpipes, **drainpipe pants**, **drainpipe trousers** full-length trousers cut very narrow in the leg and worn as tightly fitting as possible.
dates mainly 1950s as an expression; the cut has been revived several times but the later versions are more likely to be referred to as pegs, skin-tight or skinny jeans.
derivation descriptive.

Derby shoes
Leather
British, 1935–9
V&A: Misc.266&A–1979

drawers 1 knickers or underpants, usually with extended legs. 'There is a difference in the cut of drawers for girls and boys. The girl's are shorter than a boy's, by an inch at least [from waist to crotch] … and about two inches wider … across the seat. Otherwise, up to this age, they are made the same … Young girls of this age [eight years] need a little trimming on the drawers, as they show much' (*Cassell's Household Guide*, *c*.1885). Also called, euphemistically, mainly 19th century, **ineffibles** [*sic*]**, inexpressibles, nether integuments, unmentionables**

Drawers for a boy
Cotton jersey and linen
British, *c*.1850
V&A: B.931(1)–1993

2 another word for trowsers or pantalettes. 'It was the fashion then to have the drawers long, showing the double-worked frills below the hem of the dress' (Mary Haldane on the fashions of about 1830, quoted in Pollock, *A Lasting Relationship*).

dates 16th century onward for boys; about 1810 onward for girls. In later use often consciously old-fashioned or humorous.

derivation garment which the wearer draws (pulls) on.

Drawers for a girl
Cotton
British, *c*.1840
V&A: Misc.9(4)–1977

dress a garment incorporating a bodice and skirt, worn by babies, girls and women, and (up to about 1920) by young boys. *Also called* **frock** The term frock was formerly more frequently used to describe younger children's dresses (and is sometimes indicative of the fact that they were back-fastening). The Foundling Hospital checklist of 1742 uses only 'frock' for such a garment (by 1759 the list also included 'gown' and 'robe' – *see **Appendix 1**).

ballerina dress a dress with a fitted bodice and fuller than usual swirling skirt, a loose interpretation of ballet costume, fashionable for girls between the late 1940s and early 1960s.

mini dress, **maxi dress** dresses of exaggeratedly short or long lengths respectively, originally fashionable in the 1960s.

paper dress a dress made of Vilene or other similar bonded fabric, perceived as resembling paper (1960s).

dates dress was in earliest use to denote clothing in general, and the action of putting it on. The specific meaning of a particular garment appears to date from the early 18th century; frock is 17th century onward, though it was in use from the 14th century for monastic and rural garments, for example.

derivation dress from Old French *dresser* 'to arrange'; frock is from French *froc* but ultimately of uncertain origin.

dress improver *see bustle*

dress shirt *see shirt*

Opposite
Dress for a girl
Silk with velvet and lace
British, 1855
V&A: T.403–1971

Below
Dress for a boy
Velvet
British, *c.*1868
V&A: T.222–1968

Right above
Dress for a baby
Smocked silk
British, *c.*1937
V&A: Misc.219–1984

Right below
Diane Mayersohn,
paper dress
Printed vilene
British, 1967
V&A: Misc.21–1988

dressing gown (US equivalent **robe**) a coat-like garment worn between undressing and going to bed, or between getting up and dressing, formerly considered highly important for children to wear to avoid catching cold. Formerly (16th century) called **nightgown**.
kimono a Western adaptation, usually in a lightweight fabric, of the traditional Japanese garment, used as a lightweight dressing gown.
dates (this usage) 19th century to present day.
derivation originally worn during dressing.

Pasolds Ltd,
Ladybird dressing gown
Polyester
British, 1981
(older design)
V&A: Misc.143&A–1982

dressing-up clothes the informal, home-based equivalent of *fancy dress*, and more likely to consist wholly or partly of generic or improvised items. 'My keenest joy was to dress up as a fairy, with a wand made of a tall reed from the marshes at Leasoe, and to bound in upon my family from the nursery and bestow imaginary gifts upon them' (Angela Brazil [born 1868], *My Own Schooldays*, 1927).
dates recorded use from 1860s onward, but undoubtedly used earlier.
derivation from the verb *to dress* in the sense 'to put on clothing for a particular effect or purpose', also known in the phrase 'to dress [more formally] for dinner'.

dribble catcher *see bib*

drill dress *or tunic see gymslip*

Dr Martens™ brand specific footwear with a cushioned sole ('AirWair'). Originally devised by a doctor to support his injured ankle, then commercially produced as industrial and protective footwear.

It subsequently became a fashion brand, available in many styles and patterns (including floral and plaid) for adults and children, although reference to them usually indicates the original eight-eyelet lace-up boot in plain black. *Also called* **Doc Martens**, **DMs**

dates 1960 onward.

derivation named after their inventor, Dr Klaus Maertens.

Below
Dr Martens boots
Leather
British, 1980–85
V&A: B.78(1,2)–1995

Right
Butterick Ltd,
sewing pattern
for a duffel coat
Printed paper
British, 1970–79
V&A: Misc.322(1)–1987

duffel coat, **duffle coat** (USA **tow coat**, **convoy coat**) a hooded coat of thick fabric, fastening at the front with toggles and loops, popular as childrenswear especially in the 1950s and 1960s. The earliest modern examples, even for children, were of drab colours such as grey and fawn, but following the appearance of Michael Bond's Paddington Bear (book first published 1958) in his bright blue duffel coat, a variety of different colours became available.

dates coats and cloaks of duffel were available from the 17th century, but the classic form of duffel coat worn by children dates from the 1950s onward, and appears to have been introduced in Britain following its use by naval personnel in the Second World War.

derivation *duffel* or *duffle*, a thick woollen fabric originally made in the town of Duffel in Belgium.

dungarees (USA **overalls**) trousers
with a bib and shoulder straps. *Also called*
play slacks

dates originally working men's clothes,
particularly popular for children from
1920 onward.

derivation from *dungaree*, a coarse calico fabric.

dust cloak, **dust coat**, **dust gown**,
dust wrap *see overall*

OshKosh, dungarees
Cotton
USA, *c.*1984
V&A: Misc.714–1992

eE

ear cap 1 a cap with earflaps (e.g. a *deerstalker*). **2** a pair of ear covers connected by a band. **3** a close-fitting orthopaedic cap, often of mesh fabric, worn during sleep to help flatten protuberant ears, e.g. the Happy Days brand 'adjustable hygienic Ear Cap, scientifically adapted to conform to the shape of the head. Practical and effective in counteracting prominent ears'.
dates 1 & 2 1840s onward. **3** late 19th to early 20th century.
derivation descriptive.

earmuffs a pair of ear coverings on a connecting band, probably US in origin.
dates 1850s onward.
derivation descriptive.

espadrille a rope-soled canvas shoe, often with long ties, usually beach or casual wear, derived from an item of Pyrenean folk costume.
dates fashion use from late 19th century onward.
derivation French, ultimately from esparto grass originally used in its manufacture.

Espadrilles
Canvas and rope
British, *c*.1885
V&A: Misc.713(1,2)–1993

Eton collar a large, fairly deep, detachable collar of stiff white linen, worn with an *Eton suit*, but also worn by boys for formal wear as part of other types of suit. There was also a **deep Eton collar** (mentioned in Army & Navy Stores list, 1939–40).

dates the characteristic form of the Eton collar seems to date from the 1830s onward.

derivation from Eton College, boys' public school.

Gardiners,
Eton suit and collar
British, *c.*1931
V&A: B.304(1,3)–1997

Eton suit, **Etons** a short jacket and waistcoat worn with a white shirt, large stiff collar (the *Eton collar*), long grey trousers and top hat. Worn by the younger boys of Eton College and the choirboys of Henry VI's other foundation, King's College, Cambridge. It was adopted by other boys' schools, to the extent that *Punch* (4 December 1901), reporting on the probability that the Bluecoat Boys of Christ's Hospital, Horsham, would soon be allowed to 'adopt modern dress' instead of their Tudor gowns, depicted one of them in an Eton suit. The Eton suit was also worn on formal occasions by boys, including those who would not have worn the suit at school, from the 1870s to the 1930s (*see* **evening dress**).

dates late 18th century onward, but with some later modifications, e.g. the colour of the jacket changed to black on the death of George III (1820).

derivation from Eton College, boys' public school.

Boy wearing an Eton suit and collar,
by an unknown photographer
Photographic print, *c.*1900
V&A: MoC

evening dress garments of more formal or elaborate style for wear to parties, formal meals, etc. In the 19th century, boys' evening dress conventionally came to consist of a long-tailed black coat and trousers with a white shirt and black or white bow tie. In the late 1880s the less formal dinner jacket was introduced (see below). The equivalent for girls was always reflective of the prevailing fashions, but often with shorter sleeves and lower neckline. 'Girls begin to talk of their "ball dress" from the hour at which an invitation comes; boys, on the contrary, never think they want anything, until the very moment the article in question should be donned, so it is convenient to find that we can obtain, within a few minutes, collars, cuffs, white or black neckties, socks, shirts …' (*Myra's Journal*, 1 January 1879). In the early 20th century the conventional black dinner jacket and trousers were more associated with boys in their middle teens and older; for younger boys the Eton suit was often customary instead, although as late as 1939–40 the Army & Navy Stores catalogue lists evening dress for boys as young as twelve. Girls of all ages, up to the 1960s, often wore white or pastel-coloured dresses, usually more elaborately made or finished than their day clothes. *Also called* **party clothes**, **party dress**

dinner jacket a jacket without tails, for less formal evening wear. Originally known as a 'dress lounge', the term 'dinner jacket' was in use from 1898 onward. In Elinor M. Brent-Dyer's novel *Seven Scamps* (1927), Rex, who is sixteen, has a dinner jacket for formal evening wear, but thirteen-year-old Peter still wears an Eton suit.

tuxedo, **tuxedo coat**, **tuxedo jacket** US name for dinner jacket or dinner suit (from Tuxedo Park, New York, site of the country club where it was first worn).

dates for children, the concept of evening dress originates in the 1840s and '50s with the rise of children's parties.

derivation descriptive.

Creation brand,
evening dress suit
Polyester
British, c.2000
V&A: MoC

Fair Isle knitwear traditional Fair Isle knitwear has bands of complex patterns, often five or more different bands to a sequence. In childrenswear it was often made in other parts of Britain, either commercially or by using knitting patterns designed for the domestic knitter. The bands on these latter garments were usually narrower and much more repetitive, giving a striped effect, particularly where the motifs were small in scale.

dates particularly characteristic of 1930–59. Richard Rutt in *A History of Hand Knitting* (1987) dates Fair Isle knitting of jumpers to 1890 at the earliest, and in multicoloured yarns as we know it to the 1920s.

derivation Fair Isle, one the Shetland Islands, where the style originated.

Fair Isle cap
Knitted wool
Scottish, *c*.1955
V&A: Misc.23(1)–1987

fall front a fastening for trousers or breeches that opens and closes with a squared button-through flap below the waist.

whole falls or a **whole fall front** extends the full width of the trouser front, **small** or **split falls** or a **small** or **split fall front** describes a narrower central flap.

dates 1730s–1860s for boys.

derivation presumably because the flap falls when undone.

falling collar *see collar*

Whole fall front
on trousers
Cotton
British, late 19th century
V&A: Misc.352–1979

Bottom
Small fall front
on trousers
Nankeen
British, early
19th century
V&A: T.165(A)–1915

fancy dress an imaginative form of costume to represent the wearer as something or someone else, for an organized occasion such as a party or competition. Fancy-dress parties derived from the 18th- and early 19th-century masquerade tradition, where a participant would wear a mask and a voluminous cloak called a domino as a disguise. Fancy-dress costumes were more specific. Popular costumes for children include fictional characters, flowers and creatures, historical and national costumes, and topical or humorous outfits. Ardern Holt's *Fancy Dresses Described, or What to Wear at Fancy Balls* (1879), one of the earliest publications to suggest costume options, included a section on those suitable for boys and girls as well as adults. Charlotte Corday and Napoleon are on her list of suggestions for children, as well as the more obvious characters from nursery rhymes and children's literature.
dates 1840s to the present day. Children's fancy-dress parties rose to popularity in the mid-19th century. They were held by Queen Victoria and Prince Albert in the 1840s and '50s, the Prince and Princess of Wales in 1874, and the Marchioness of Salisbury in the mid-1870s, for example. The Lord Mayor of London's annual fancy-dress ball for children goes back in an unbroken tradition to 1883 (see pp.6, 183).
derivation from the *fancy* of the wearer to appear in a particular guise.

Daniel Neal Ltd,
jockey fancy dress
Cotton
British, 1925–30
V&A: Misc.320–1978

Fauntleroy suit, Little Lord Fauntleroy suit a historicizing costume for boys, typically including a lace collar and a tunic or jacket and knee breeches of velvet. The style was originally based on 17th-century dress, but sometimes incorporated other historical elements, such as a Tudor bonnet.
dates the form of the suit pre-dates the novel, and its specific format probably arose in the 1860s as part of *Vandyke dress*. Dilute forms of the Fauntleroy suit, in the form of lace collared velveteen tunics with shorts, were still being worn by some small boys in the 1910s and '20s.
derivation as worn by the eponymous hero of Frances Hodgson Burnett's best-selling novel, *Little Lord Fauntleroy*, which first appeared in serial form, and was published as a book in 1886.

Eldridge & Young,
Fauntleroy suit
Plush with machine-made lace
British, 1887
V&A: T.518&A,B–1974

feeder a larger, more substantial version of a *bib*, worn to protect the clothes of a child who is eating (usually solid or semi-solid food). A feeder is usually square or rectangular, and sometimes has sleeves attached to give a closer fit and better protection.

dates probably 1880s onward.

derivation descriptive (worn during feeding) but possibly also connected with the same word applied to a spoon, commonly used to feed young children.

feely boppers see *deely bobbers*

Feeder
Embroidered linen
British, *c.*1928
V&A: Misc.13(5)–1977

fichu a triangular wrap placed around the neck and shoulders and across the chest, usually contained within the neckline of a dress.

dates originally 18th century, revived in the 1890s to wear over a dress bodice.

derivation French for a small shawl or headscarf, possibly from the verb *ficher*, in the sense of dressed, covered; the OED suggests another sense of *fichu*: 'put on carelessly'.

First Communion clothes see *Confirmation outfit*

first shirt see *shirt*

fishtail parka see *parka*

Fichu from doll
Cotton
British, *c.*1800
V&A: T.134–1926

fishwife dress a type of girl's short-skirted dress with striped overskirt and trimmings, probably becoming popular as an adjunct of the various nautical costumes that were fashionable in the late 19th century. In 1876 Debenham & Freebody advertised it as 'a novel costume', offering a version with an apron and basket for £1 5s (*Myra's Journal*, 1 May 1876).
dates mainly 1870s–90s.
derivation based on the costume of Scots fishergirls and women.

flannel *see barracoat*

flares, **flared trousers** trousers, close fitting to the knee and then cut noticeably wider to the ankle. At the height of its popularity in the 1970s, the flared cut was even in evidence in children's pyjamas and babies' dungarees.
dates flared trousers were traditionally associated with sailors' clothing (*see bell bottoms*), but became a fashion staple of the period 1965–75 in particular. *See also loons*
derivation: descriptive (the verb *to flare* is of unknown origin).

flashlight trainer *see trainer*

Debenham & Freebody advertisement for a fishwife dress
Printed paper
British, 1876
V&A: MoC

fleece a jacket, sweatshirt or similar garment, usually made from synthetic fleece fabric.
dates 1990s onward.
derivation from its resemblance to *fleece* in its original sense, the skin of a sheep or similar creature (Old English *fléos,* of Germanic origin).

flip-flop a sandal, usually made of plastic or rubber, consisting of a sole with a V-shaped strap attached to a toe-post near the front, based on the sandals worn with traditional Japanese costume. In contemporary use, flip-flops are also made in fur fabric or towelling for use as slippers.
dates 1960s onward.
derivation from the movement or sound of the shoe produced when walking.

flower girl's dress *see bridesmaid's dress*

Flip-flops
Plastic
Hong Kong, *c.*1981
V&A: Misc.50(1,2)–1982

fly, **fly front**, informally **flies** a trouser fastening, usually button-through, with a flap of the fabric over the fastening.

dates on trousers, 1840s onward.

derivation the OED gives one meaning of 'fly' as 'something attached by the edge', but this use of the word is ultimately of obscure origin.

flying suit *see jumpsuit*

Fly front on trousers
Wool
British, 1856
V&A: T.70(B)–1929

fontange a girl's or woman's headdress consisting of a linen cap with a high-standing lace – or lace and fabric – frill in front, often with a pair of matching **lappets** (streamers) hanging from the back. For the youngest girls an upstanding frill at the front of the cap or undercap was sometimes deemed enough. An example of a child wearing a fontange can be seen in the portrait by Nicolas de Largillière of James II's youngest daughter, Princess Louisa Maria Teresa, with her brother James in 1695 (National Portrait Gallery, London).

dates 1680s–1700s, although apparently already considered old fashioned in some quarters by 1699.

derivation from Marie Angélique de Scorailles de Roussille, Duchesse de Fontanges (1661–81), who was briefly a mistress of Louis XIV of France. When her hair came down during a hunt, she is said to have tied it up with a garter, finishing in a bow at the front, a look which the King found attractive and which was quickly copied and considerably elaborated upon.

Fontange for the
'Old Pretender' doll
Muslin with lace
and ribbon
English, 1680s
V&A: W.18–1945

football strip the distinctive clothing worn on the pitch during a match to identify the members of a football team (shirt or jersey, shorts and socks). Many teams market versions of their strips in adults' and children's sizes for supporters to buy.

dates as an expression, 1970s onward, although the concept is basically 19th century.

derivation uncertain, but possibly from the sense of 'to strip' (take off normal clothes) for play, from Middle High German *strupfen*.

forage cap *see* **cap**

forehead cloth a triangular piece of fabric which literally crosses over the head or forehead, worn beneath a cap or caps (included as part of the swaddling clothes layette).

Also called **crosscloth**

dates late 16th century to late 18th century.

derivation descriptive.

foundation garment *see* **corset**

frock *see* **dress**, **coat**

Football strip
Nylon
USA, *c.*1975
V&A: Misc.592–1992

Forehead cloth
Linen
British, *c.*1700
V&A: Misc.323(2)–1984

furs furs for children have traditionally been less valuable animal skins, such as lamb (notably astrakhan), rabbit or seal. By the 20th century, fur garments (as opposed to accessories) were often for under-fives of either gender, or for girls. 'Miriam … did look very smart. She had on a white ermine coat …', although her mother goes on to explain that it only looks smart in the dimly lit surroundings, being too small and discoloured, but has to last for the war: 'We've no coupons for another' (Noel Streatfeild, *Curtain Up*, 1944). The most general form of animal pelt worn by children was sheepskin (the skin of a sheep with the fleece on the inside) which was much cheaper and harder-wearing than fur.

It was traditionally worn by children working outdoors, and has been recently fashionable in the form of the **shearling coat** and other garments, made so that the edge of the fleece shows on the outside of the seams.

dates from ancient times to the present day, although real fur for children has been largely out of favour since the 1980s. 'Fun furs', made of fur fabrics in unlikely colours, were fashionable in the 1960s.

derivation probably Old French *forre, fuerre* 'sheath or case'. A 'shearling' is the first fleece shorn from a lamb, a term in use since the medieval period.

Fur cape
Rabbit skin lined with satin
British, c.1890
V&A: Misc.1019–1992

g G

gabrielle dress *see princess coat*

gaiter a knee-length or just over knee-length leg covering for outdoor wear, for children usually fastening with buttons or buckled straps, and resembling a sole-less boot with a strap under the instep (in 20th century childrenswear, the strap was often of elastic). 'Mr. Bird, of Oxford Street, showed me a very nice gaiter which he has had made for young ladies, and which no school-girl should be without' (*Myra's Journal*, 2 October 1876).

spatterdash a long gaiter, worn to keep trousers or stockings clean.

spat (abbreviation of *spatterdash*) an early 19th century to mid-20th century shorter version of the spatterdash, coming to just above the ankle.

dates late 18th century onward; still sometimes in use for children in the 1950s

derivation the OED online has French *guêtre*, *guietre*, but of unknown origin; *spatterdash* is a compound of *spatter* and *dash*, both of which include meanings to splash with water, mud, etc.

galosh, **golosh** (many other variations) *galosh* was originally a general term for an item of footwear, much as 'shoe' is. In the 19th century it became a rubber overshoe, worn to protect footwear in wet or muddy conditions. 'In wet or dirty weather India rubber over-shoes are useful, as they keep the *upper* as well as the *under* leathers perfectly dry' (Pye Henry Chavasse, *Advice to a Mother*, 1870). Some galoshes reached further up the foot or had a 'storm' front or flap in the front for greater protection. *Also called* **rubber**, **overshoe**

dates rubber galoshes were patented in the 1840s. They were still listed in the children's footwear section of the *Army & Navy Stores Catalogue* for 1939–40, but would have become scarce with the fall of the major rubber-producing area of Singapore in 1942, and were not reintroduced after the Second World War.

derivation French *galoche* from the Greek for a shoemaker's last.

Galoshes for a doll
Moulded rubber
USA, 1920–39
V&A: B.12 (1,2)–1998

Koziephit brand, gaiters
Fleece-backed cotton
British, *c.*1925
V&A: Misc.87(1,2)–1984

garibaldi blouse, **garibaldi bodice**, **garibaldi jacket**, **garibaldi shirt** a woman's or girl's garment, originally of scarlet cloth, sometimes trimmed with black braid, with wrist-length sleeves. The blouse or shirt was generally fairly close-fitting and cinched at the waist with a belt, whereas the bodice and jacket were of looser cut. Because of the popularity of the fashion, there were many variations in its form and colour.

dates 1860s.

derivation based on the red shirts worn by the Italian nationalist General Giuseppe Garibaldi (1807–82) and his followers. Garibaldi visited England in 1854 and 1863, adding greatly to his popularity there.

Garibaldi jacket (variation)
Embroidered wool
British, c.1860
V&A: Misc.770–1986

garter a band of woven or knitted fabric, sometimes of decorative appearance, worn around the leg to hold up a stocking, and the only device for doing so until the introduction of the various types of **suspender**. 'I should advise a boy to wear socks, not stockings; as he will then be able to dispense with garters. Garters … are injurious – they not only interfere with the circulation of the blood, but also, by pressure, injure the bones, and thus the shape of the legs' (Pye Henry Chavasse, *Advice to a Mother,* 1870). Until the introduction of elastic, in order to perform its function, the garter had to be fastened quite tightly about the leg, hence the concern about circulation; even so it would tend to work loose and need to be retied.

dates Middle Ages onward. Simple garters made of broad elastic were still in use among schoolchildren in the 1960s and '70s.

derivation Old French *gartier* from *garet* 'the bend of the knee'.

garter belt *see **suspender belt***

gauze square *see **nappy liner***

Garters for a doll
Knitted wool
British, 1900
V&A: T.186–1931

gender indicators factors such as the wearing of skirts or the styling and length of hair are not reliable indicators of gender when looking at representations of children.

accoutrements a child holding a whip, a drum or any kind of weapon is likelier to be a boy than a girl. A child holding flowers or any domestic item is likely to be a girl. Fruit and animals are held by children of both sexes.

alignment as well as the positioning of a *cockade*, hair partings have been associated with boys when on the right and girls when on the left, but centre partings were worn by both (and US naïve paintings tend to show side partings for boys and centre partings for girls), but this varies with date.

buttoning the convention for button-through fastening at the front of a boy's garment is left-over-right; for girls it is right-over-left.

colour 'pink for a girl, blue for a boy' is a 20th-century practice, probably assisted by the marketing industry. In pre-1800 children's clothing the reverse is often true, and in Roman Catholic cultures, blue is associated with the Virgin Mary and therefore particularly suitable for a girl, whereas pink is sometimes seen as a version of red, associated with St Joseph, and therefore suggesting a boy.

gilet 1 a sleeveless jacket, often of waterproof and/or padded material. **2** a dress bodice shaped like a waistcoat.

dates 1 1970s onward. **2** late 19th century.

derivation French for waistcoat.

gipsy cloak *see cloak*

Girl Guide uniform *see Appendix 2*

Girls' Brigade *see Appendix 2*

Tesco Stores Ltd, gilet
Nylon
British/Korean, 1983
V&A: Misc.406–1984

glengarry, **glengarry bonnet** a close-fitting cap, higher at the front, with a central pleat from the front to the back of the head, often decorated with a large feather at one side and pendant ribbons at the back; often worn with the *Scotch suit*.

dates 1860s onward, still sometimes worn by children as part of occasion dress.

derivation from Glengarry, a valley in Scotland.

Isaac Walton & Co.,
glengarry bonnet
Velvet with metal,
ribbon and feather trim
British, 1865–75
V&A: Misc.351(6)–1979

glove a close-fitting covering for the entire hand, with distinct spaces for fingers and thumb; made in more substantial fabrics such as leather and wool for warmth in cold weather, but also historically in lightweight fabrics in warmer weather, particularly in a formal context (white gloves were still worn by girls for best in summer as late as the early 1960s).

dates 12th century onward.

derivation from Old English *glóf*.

golosh *see galosh*

Gloves
Chamois leather
French, 1920–29
V&A: B.147(1,2)–1999

Bottom
Gloves
Crocheted cotton mesh
French, 1925–35
V&A: B.947(1,2)–1993

gown, **robe** once the more usual names for a dress, but now more or less obsolete except for formal wear, such as 'ball gown' and 'christening robe'; their former everyday use in children's clothing is evident in nursery rhymes and riddles such as 'Daffy-down-dilly is new come to town, With a yellow petticoat, and a green gown' (first printed 1805).

mantua a front-fastening gown with a train and unstiffened bodice, worn by girls and women from about 1650 to 1750.

sack, **sack-back**, **sacque** in the 18th century, a gown with a 'sack-back' – a pair of box-pleats in the fabric of the back of the dress, which were caught down with stitching a few inches below the neck and then allowed to fall loose to the hem.

dates 14th century onward (the word 'gown' also originally included a loose coat-like male garment which survives as the academic gown).

derivation *gown* is of debated origin, possibly from Old French *goune* from Latin *gunna*, 'fur garment'; *robe* is from Old French *robe*; the origin of *mantua* has been obscured by the fact that while some of the gowns may have been made of mantua fabric, named after the Italian city of the same name, in other cases there seems to have been a confusion with the French *manteau*, 'coat'.

Gown
Silk embroidered in China
British-made garment, *c*.1760
V&A: T.183–1965

grandad shirt *see shirt*

greatcoat *see coat*

Greenaway style *see Kate Greenaway*

grip *see hairgrip*

g-string *see thong*

guernsey, **guernsey shirt** *see jersey*

Guide uniform, **Girl Guide uniform**
see Appendix 2

gumboot, **gum-boot** *see wellington boot*

gymslip, **gym tunic**, **gymnasium dress**, **gymmer**, **drill dress**, **drill tunic**, **tunic** originally a short, sleeveless overdress, worn by girls over a blouse or shirt for physical education, subsequently adopted as daywear, in particular for school uniform. There are two main types, the earlier one with box pleats falling from a squared yoke and tied with a sash, the later version with a fitted bodice and flared skirt. The gymslip probably also led to the widespread use of the *pinafore dress*.

dates 19th century to present day. Introduced by Madame Bergman Osterberg, Head of Dartford College for Physical Training in 1885.

derivation abbreviation of 'gymnastics tunic'.

Gymslip
Serge, with cotton blouse
British, *c.*1935
V&A: Misc.318(1,2)–1984

habit shirt *see shirt*

hacking jacket, **hacking coat** a tailored single-breasted riding jacket with long sleeves, often in checked fabric.

dates 1940s onward; a fashion item in the 1970s.

derivation originally worn for *hacking*, riding a horse in an informal context.

Hacking jacket
Wool blend
British, 1975–81
V&A: Misc.438–1981

hairband, **headband** a head-sized loop of elasticated or elastic-linked or stiffened fabric, or a plastic or metal arch (sometimes fabric covered), worn to hold the hair off the face.

Also called **Alice band**, **bandeau**

dates the form was in use from at least the 1450s.

derivation hairband, headband descriptive; Alice band from Tenniel's illustrations to Lewis Carroll's *Through the Looking Glass and What Alice Found There* (1871); *bandeau* from French *bande*, *bandel*, 'band'.

Hairband
Moulded plastic
British, *c.*1960
V&A: Misc.264–1981

hairgrip (US **bobby pin**) a sprung clip (basically a folded strip of metal) for holding the hair in place. *Also called* **kirbigrip™**, **kirby grip**, **grip**

dates hairgrip or hair-grip has been in use as a term since at least the 1890s.

derivation descriptive; the *kirby grip* was the creation of Kirby, Beard & Co. Ltd of Birmingham, who also made safety pins; *bobby pin* is of uncertain origin but probably connected with the bob hairstyle.

Hairgrips with bows
Metal and ribbon
British, 1930–35
V&A: Misc.143(2,3)–1984

Slides
Plastic and metal
British, 1940–49
V&A: Misc.233–1988 (part)

hairslide, **slide** (US **barrette**) a hinged or sprung clip, sometimes decorative, for holding the hair in place.

slide comb a hinged comb, generally circular, to hold the hair in place in a ponytail or each of a pair of bunches.

dates 1890s onward; *slides* were originally in general use as clasps, often for use with clothing, and date back at least another hundred years.

derivation descriptive; from Old English *slídan*, 'slide'.

hamster sock *see sock*

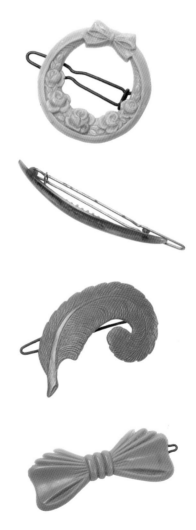

handbag a bag for small personal items, to carry by hand. Its immediate predecessors were the reticule (or ridicule) and the dorothy bag, but it ultimately derived from the *pocket*.
dates 1850s onward.
derivation descriptive.

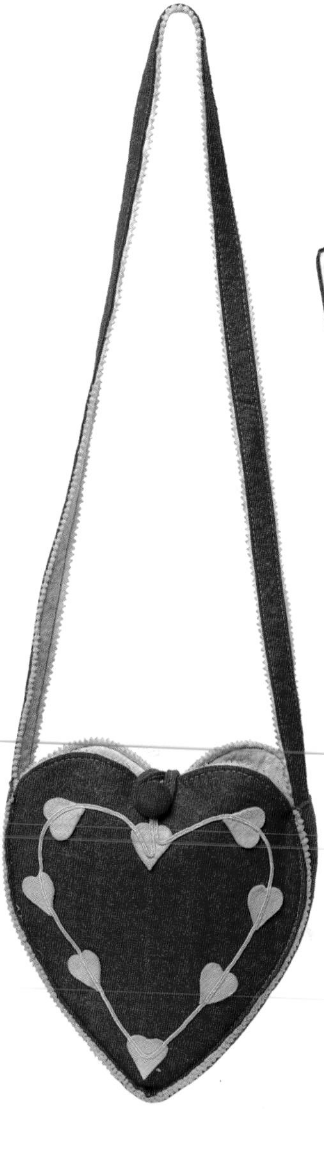

Shoulder bag
Appliquéd felt
USA, 1945–55
V&A: B.131–1995

handkerchief, **hankercher** (dialect), informally **hankie**, **hanky** a piece of fabric for wiping the nose or face; sometimes called a pocket handkerchief to distinguish it from handkerchief used in the sense of a neck covering.
dates 16th century onward.
derivation literally hand (held) kerchief, from Middle English *coverchef, keverchef* from Old French *couvrechief, cuevrechief*, from *couvrir*, 'cover', *chief*, 'head'.

Handkerchief
Printed cotton
British, 1960–69
V&A: Misc.184(2)–1988

Handbag
Embroidered canvas
with silk cord
British, c.1840
V&A: Misc.9(20)–1977

hand-me-down a second-hand (or third-hand or more) garment, often, though not necessarily, inherited from an older member of the family. Hand-me-downs were sometimes the only way for a child to have enough clothes, particularly if times were hard for a family, if there were many children to clothe, or widespread shortages, as in the Second World War. 'By dint of buying some extra organdie and letting out, and adding some frills, Nana had succeeded in making the frocks Pauline and Petrova had bought for "A Midsummer Night's Dream" audition do for Petrova and Posy' (Noel Streatfeild, *Ballet Shoes*, 1936). The use of hand-me-downs has also long been considered normal in upper-class families.

dates earliest printed mention OED: 1874; still in use.

derivation descriptive.

Marie Anna Kuehn
wearing a hat
Photographic print
British, 1904
V&A: MoC

With best wishes

Augustus Young,
Wellington Road

hat a generic name now applied to virtually any headgear, but originally implying one with a crown and a brim.

bowler hat (US **derby hat**) one with a domed crown and curving brim; sometimes associated with hunting.

top hat a tall cylindrical hat with a curving brim, associated with the *Eton suit*.

dates from ancient times onward; there was something of an expectation that everyone, even the poor, would wear a hat or cap of some kind out of doors. 'Males and females alike, we had always to wear something on our heads out of doors. Even for children playing in the garden, this was absolutely necessary. According to the weather, we were told that we should catch cold, or get sunstroke, if we went bareheaded. But the real reason was that it was proper – that the hat was an essential part of the dress' (G. Raverat [born 1885], *Period Piece*, 1954). This expectation began to die out in the Second World War, and was finally killed off during the 1960s. It was not that hats were not fashionable then, for they were, but they were not essential in the same kind of way, especially for the young.

derivation Old English *hæt*.

head scarf, headscarf *see scarf*

Boy wearing a bowler hat, from *The London Art Fashions*
Fashion plate, 1889
V&A: E.1424–1946

heely™ (plural **heelys**) a trainer with a roller embedded in the heel. The wearer can glide by putting the whole foot on the ground and transferring their weight to the heel, but has to walk or run on tiptoe. Subsequently banned in some places on safety grounds. *Also called* **streetglider**

dates fashionable among British children from 2006 onward, but shoes with wheels embedded were available in some countries as early as the 1980s and '90s.

derivation from the emphasis on the heel when used.

Highland suit *see Scotch suit*

Heelys
Nylon and plastic
British, 2007
V&A: MoC Collections

hood a loose-fitting head cover of fabric, or later sometimes knitted. 'A white hood for Katy and a blue one for Clover, both of … [their younger sister Elsie's] own knitting' (S. Coolidge, *What Katy Did at School,* set 1868–9); in later childrenswear, often attached to a coat or jacket.

hoodie 1 a hooded jacket or sweatshirt of soft fabric such as fleece, popular in Britain from the 1990s. **2** a person wearing a hoodie, notably with the hood up.

woodie hoodie a hooded top designed and worn by young members of Woodcraft Folk (see **Appendix 2**).

dates Middle Ages onward.

derivation From Old English *hód*.

Hood
Velvet with ribbon
and silver lace
Alsace-Lorraine,
18th century
V&A: B.89–1993

hoop, **hooped petticoat** a ring or frame for extending the skirts of a gown, or a petticoat with concentric rings of rigid material such as wire, whalebone or cane.

dates mainly 18th century in Britain, but apparently in longer use, particularly in the US, as a synonym for the crinoline type of petticoat. 'We asked Grandmother if we could have some hoop skirts like the seminary girls and she said no, we were not old enough' (Caroline Richards, aged ten in 1852, quoted in Linda Pollock, *A Lasting Relationship*, 1987). Caroline's seven-year-old sister Anna attempted to achieve the effect by running a reed through the hem of her skirt, but Caroline commented: 'She wouldn't want to [wear it] if she knew how terrible it looked.'

derivation from Old English *hóp*.

hose, **hosiery** a collective name for **socks**, **stockings**, **tights**. 'Mr Jannings also supplies children's silk hosiery in white, pink, and blue silk … these are ribbed and so will keep up better over fat little legs' (*Myra's Journal*, 1 December 1879).

hot pants women's or girls' shorts of exaggerated cut, tighter and shorter than usual.

dates early 1970s.

derivation from Old English *hát*.

Emu Wools Ltd, knitting pattern for hot pants
Printed paper
British, 1970–79
V&A: Misc.61(20)–1990

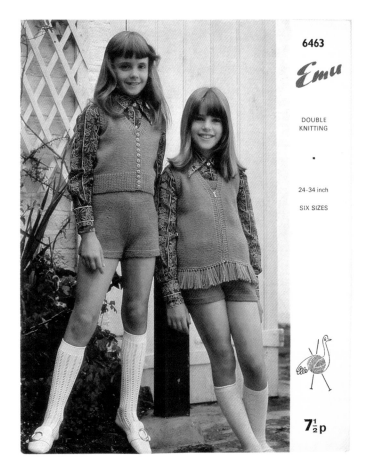

6463

Emu

DOUBLE KNITTING

•

24-34 inch

SIX SIZES

$7\frac{1}{2}$p

housecoat, **house gown**, **house dress**, **house frock** **1** originally an informal coat-dress for wearing at home. **2** a dressing gown, often quilted.
dates **1** 1830s onward. **2** 1950s onward.
derivation descriptive.

hug-me-tight *see shawl*

Erica brand, housecoat
Printed nylon
British, 1964–5
V&A: Misc.152–1985

hussar dress clothing taking its inspiration from the flamboyant uniforms of the hussar cavalry regiments, which typically included frogging, braid, tassels and sashes, and the use of contrasting colours. Elaborately trimmed and exaggeratedly styled caps for boys were one of the most widespread forms of the fashion, but hussar influence was to be seen in a variety of garments for children, including dresses for girls and younger boys.
dates 1800–1835.
derivation from Hungarian *huszar*, originally 'pirate, robber'.

Hussar suit
Cotton
British, *c.*1835
V&A: T.15&A,B–1944

iI jJ

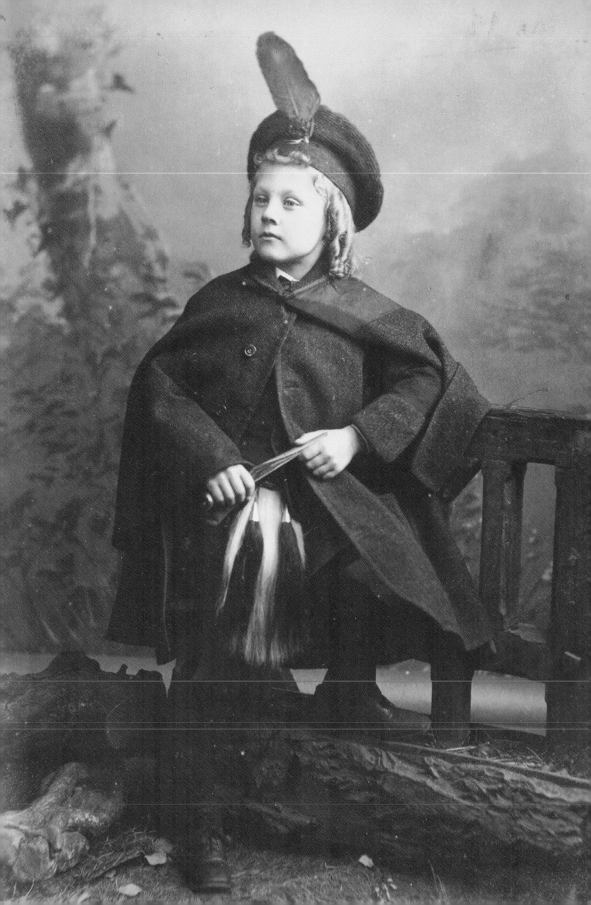

ineffibles, **inexpressibles** mainly 19th-century euphemisms for **trousers** or **drawers**

infantee *see mitten*

Inverness, **Inverness cape**, **Inverness cloak**, **Inverness coat**
a short, loose-fitting man's or boy's outdoor coat with wide sleeves and a cape. The cape was sometimes incomplete at the back and stitched into the seams.
dates 1860s–90s.
derivation from the Scottish town.

jack tar suit *see sailor suit*

Opposite
Sepia albumen print
of Justin Laczkovic
wearing an Inverness
English, 1881
V&A: B.82(17)–1995

jacket a short outer coat with sleeves, front-fastening in single or double breasted – or occasionally asymmetrical – cut. In modern usage the word can apply equally to indoor wear, as in the jacket of a suit, or outdoor wear, as in the bomber jacket. *See also* **blazer**, *hacking jacket*
blouson a short jacket shaped like a blouse, recorded as early as 1904, but more characteristic of the 1950s onward.
bomber jacket a short jacket with zip fastener and knitted cuffs and welt, inspired by the leather jackets worn by USAF air-crews in the Second World War.
Nehru jacket a long jacket with wrist-length sleeves and a straight edged stand-up collar, fashionable from the 1960s onward, and named after those worn by Jawaharlal Nehru (1889–1964), Prime Minister of India 1947–64.
windcheater a wind-resistant jacket, popular from the 1950s onward.
dates 1370s onward.
derivation Old French *ja(c)quet*.

Jacket (bomber jacket)
Nylon
British, 1983
V&A: Misc.407–1984

jeans trousers made of jean or denim fabric, rather like 'cords' for corduroy trousers. Jean and denim are both hardwearing fabrics, formerly used for working clothes, furnishings and boots. *Also called* **denims**

dates jeans as a garment are recorded from the 1840s onward (the fabric much earlier); denim breeches as early as 1703.

derivation *jean* from the Italian city of Genoa; *denim* from *serge de Nîmes*, 'serge from the French town of Nîmes'.

Splinter brand, jeans
Denim
British, 1990–95
V&A: B.271–1997

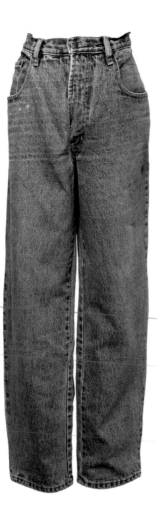

jelly, **jelly shoe**, **jelly sandal** a soft, often translucent plastic shoe for beach or casual wear.

dates 1970s onward.

derivation like (dessert) jelly, abbreviation of gelatine, which gives something of the stiffness of things which are frozen, derived from Middle English *gelé* from French *gelée* from Latin *gelata*.

jelly welly *see* **wellington boot**

jerkin originally a close-fitting male garment. In childrenswear **1** a sleeveless jacket or tunic. **2** a sideless waistcoat on a waistband.

dates particularly fashionable in the 1950s and 1960s.

derivation of unknown origin.

Sunysan brand, jelly shoe
Moulded plastic
British, 1983
V&A: Misc.546(1,2)–1985

Opposite
Pattern Practical, sewing pattern for a jerkin
Printed paper
British, 1970–79
V&A: Misc.1033–1991

No. 5535
Size: 4-6 years.

Practical

jersey a close-fitting knitted tunic (also a type of woollen yarn, and a fine machine-knitted fabric), more or less synonymous with **jumper**, **pullover**, **sweater**.

jersey suit, **jersey dress** one made of jersey fabric. 'One of the nicest presents, for Mama, is a lovely little fisherman's Jersey suit, for her tiny boy' (*Myra's Journal*, 1 December 1879).

dates 1830s onward.

derivation from the island of Jersey, which produced its own distinctive jersey yarn and various garments made from it. Similarly, **guernsey**, **guernsey shirt**, **gansey** knitted garments from the island of Guernsey. 'Master Micawber was hardly visible in a Guernsey shirt and the shaggiest suit of slops that I ever saw' (Dickens, *David Copperfield*).

jibbah, **djibbah**, **jubbah** in childrenswear, a tunic-like item of girl's clothing worn for gymnastics, eurhythmics and other forms of exercise, usually in a school context. Elizabeth Ewing discusses the jibbah in detail in her *History of Children's Costume* (1977), pp.123–4.

dates 1890s–1930s (the reference to a girl wearing a jibbah in Antonia Forest's 1948 school novel *Autumn Term* is to convey that she belongs to a family that likes to think itself artistic and unconventional).

derivation based on the long-sleeved Arab coat of the same name.

jigger coat *see coat*

Hilder & Godbold,
advertisement for jersey suits
Printed paper
British, 1881
V&A: MoC

HILDER & GODBOLD.
GIRLS' JERSEY COSTUMES,
AND
BOYS' JERSEY SUITS.

THE EASTBOURNE JERSEY COSTUME FOR GIRLS. | THE JACK TAR SUIT.

jodhpurs, informally **jodhs** ankle-length riding trousers cut exaggeratedly wide in the thigh and close-fitting from the knee down to the ankle. Sometimes worn with *jodhpur boots* *(see boot)*.

dates Western usage from late 19th century onward.

derivation based on an Indian garment, and named from the town and area of Jodhpur in Rajasthan.

Jodhpurs
Wool
French, 1939
V&A: B.122–1993

jummer probably a long or three-quarter-length dress-like garment with sleeves, similar to a *wrapping gown*.

dates 18th century. 'He had a new dress for the occasion [his brother's christening] it was a Jummer of Flower'd Gause [gauze] pleated over Blue Lutestring [lustring, a type of silk]', Lady Shelburne wrote of her son Lord Fitzmaurice, shortly before his third birthday in 1768.

derivation based on the Indian *jama(h)*, a garment of this type.

jumper 1 a knitted tunic top, more or less synonymous with *jersey*, *pullover*, *sweater*.
2 (US) a sleeveless overdress (equivalent of British *pinafore dress*).
dates possibly as early as 1908. 'Some five years ago the fashion-mongers gave the name of jumper to the knitted blouses ladies had been wearing under the name of sports coats' (*Notes and Queries*, 14 June 1930, quoted in OED).
derivation probably from French *jup*, *juppe*, from Arabic *(d)jibbah*.

Jumper
Knitted wool
European, 1925–30
V&A: Misc.554–1986

jumpsuit as a fashion item, especially for children, a sleeveless or short sleeved all-in-one garment with trouser legs, in a lightweight fabric. *Also called* **bubblesuit**, **catsuit**, **flying suit**
dates 1940s onward, but in children's clothing particularly characteristic of the 1960s onward.
derivation a one-piece suit originally worn by those making a parachute jump (or flying a plane, in the case of flying suit); the bubble suit referred to its fuller cut, whereas the cat suit was tighter fitting, and probably thought to make the wearer move like a cat.

Flying suit
Polyester and cotton blend
Hong Kong, 1984
V&A: Misc.619–1984

kK

kaftan, **caftan** a long loose-fitting tunic-like garment with wide sleeves. In Western countries a fashion garment, usually of colourful fabric, based on the Middle Eastern original.
dates particularly popular as a fashion in the 1960s and '70s.
derivation from Turkish *qaftan*.

kagoul(e), **cagoule** a lightweight waterproof tunic with long sleeves and hood, particularly in use by those taking part in outdoor activities such as hill walking; cagoules also achieved widespread usage by schoolchildren because they can be packed into a small space in a satchel or school bag.
dates 1950s onward.
derivation French *cagoule*, 'cowl'.

kamak, **kamik** see *mukluk*

Peter Storm Ltd, kagoule
Nylon
British, *c.*1980
V&A: Misc.531–1984

Kate Greenaway dress, **Kate Greenaway style** based on the illustrations of Kate Greenaway (1846–1901), who preferred to depict children in either the formal clothes of 1700 to 1780, or the radically different fashions of 1780 to 1835, rather than the contemporary clothing of her own era. The main inspiration for 'Kate Greenaway' styles came from the fashions of 1780 to 1835, with their high-waisted gowns, bonnets and mittens for girls and skeleton suits, peaked caps and frilled shirts for boys, although the *polonaise* skirts of the earlier period also had a certain amount of popularity. These styles survived into the 20th century in fancy dress, since they tended to be chosen by subsequent nursery rhyme illustrators for their characters, and in the clothes for bridesmaids and pages at weddings.
dates 1880s onward.
derivation eponymous.

kerchief see *scarf*

Kate Greenaway-style
bridesmaid's dress
Silk and chiffon
British, *c.*1926
V&A: Misc.105–1984

kilt a short pleated skirt with wrapover apron front, derived from the 'little kilt', the filibeg or philibeg (Gaelic *feileadhbeag*) of Highland Scottish dress, as opposed to the kilt formed from the folded and belted plaid.

brace kilt a kilt with shoulder straps, for children.

kilt pin, **blanket pin** a large enclosed looped pin for fastening a kilt.

dates traditional Highland use; worn by girls in the rest of Britain in the 20th century.

derivation of Scandinavian origin, perhaps from Old Norse *kilting, kjalta*, 'skirt, lap'.

kimono *see **dressing gown***

Kilt and sporran
Wool, leather
British, 1960–65
V&A: Misc.907(1–4)–1992

kippah a skullcap worn by male Orthodox Jews, and by other male Jews for religious occasions. *Also caled* **koppel**, **yarmulke**

dates traditional.

derivation *kippah* is Hebrew for 'cap'; *koppel* and *yarmulke* are Yiddish, the latter from Polish *jarmulka*, 'cap'.

kipper tie *see **tie***

kirby grip *see **hairgrip***

knapkenette *see **nappy***

knee breeches *see **breeches***

Kilt pin
Mild pressed steel
British, 1920–29
V&A: Misc.11(3)–1993

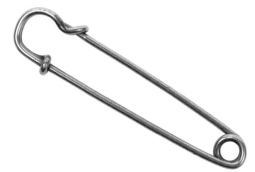

knickerbockers 1 short trousers for men and boys, usually gathered at the knee. Boys' versions also included the non-gathered style, sometimes known as **Danish trousers**.
plus twos, **plus fours** longer and wider version of knickerbockers (by two or four inches respectively). Originally associated with golfing, they were also fashion wear for older boys and men during the 1930s. **2** women's or girls' bifurcated garments, for wear beneath skirts for cycling, etc.: 'bicycling became the smart thing … we were then promoted to wearing baggy knickerbockers under our frocks, and over our white frilly drawers. We thought this horridly improper, but rather grand' (G. Raverat, born 1885, *Period Piece*, 1954).
dates 1860s to late 1930s. The Army & Navy Stores list for 1939–40 includes knickerbockers in the form of plus four suits for boys, but they would have been impossible to produce under the 1941 Utility Regulations, which banned the unnecessary use of fabric. They were never reintroduced for general wear after the Second World War.
derivation from Diedrich Knickerbocker, the pseudonym Washington Irving used in writing his *History of New York* (first published 1809). The illustrations of the original Dutch settlers of New Amsterdam (New York) show them in similar breeches.

knickers 1 underpants, originally often made from flannel, wool, or similar substantial fabrics, later a generic name mainly for women's and girls' underpants. *Also called* **pants**, **briefs**. **2** young children's shorts, particularly those for boys. **3** abbreviation of *knickerbockers*.
directoire knickers long knickers. Those made by Chilprufe in the 1920s were for girls to wear in the gymnasium and on the playing field.
knicker linings linings, usually of thin white linen or cotton, worn under woollen knickers because they were more washable. The stage and film designer Julia Trevelyan Oman (1930–2003) recalled in conversation with the author that her school knicker linings were made from her father's baby robes, and rustled as she walked because of the residual starch in the fabric.
dates 1890s onward. Shortly afterwards, knicker linings were introduced, but were another item which did not survive the rationing of the Second World War, and later became unnecessary with the introduction of more washable fabrics.
derivation knickers, abbreviation of *knickerbockers*; pants, abbreviation of *pantaloons*; briefs, descriptive.

kombat trousers *see trousers*

koppel *see kippah*

Davis & Goodman,
knickerbockers
Velvet
British, *c.*1865
V&A: T.82(B)–1970

Utility Scheme,
knickers for a girl
Knitted cotton fabric
British, 1942–52
V&A: Misc.585–1985

Marigold brand,
waterproof knickers
for a baby
Plastic
British, 1978–9
V&A: Misc.278–1981

lederhosen leather shorts traditionally worn by men and boys in Alpine regions such as the Austrian Tyrol. Although not part of the Hitler Youth movement uniform, they were generally approved of within Nazi circles because of their 'folk' associations.

dates traditional folk costume.

derivation German *leder*, 'leather', *hosen*, 'trousers'.

Opposite
Lederhosen
Leather
German, 1960–69
Misc.1247(2–5)–1991

H&M brand,
leggings for a girl
Polyamide/elastane
Swedish/Italian, 2007
V&A: MoC

H&M brand,
leggings for a girl
Cotton/elastane
Swedish/Latvian, 2007
V&A: MoC

leggings, **legginettes 1** a baby's baggy trouser-like garment with closed feet, often of knitted wool, generally for outdoor wear, possibly deriving from the fabric gaiters worn by young children. **2** women's or girls' close-fitting ankle-length trousers of jersey knit or other similar stretch fabric, with an elasticated waist, possibly derived from dancers' footless tights or the lower half of a tracksuit.

dates 1 approximately 1900 onward. **2** as a fashion item, 1980s onward.

derivation from *leg*.

leg warmer a footless tubular covering for the lower leg, usually knitted, sometimes with a 'stirrup' under the foot, and worn concertinaed towards the ankle.
dates as a fashion item, particularly characteristic of the 1980s, when it inspired a similar way of wearing socks; revived in the early years of the 21st century.
derivation descriptive, originally worn by dancers during practice or rehearsal to keep leg muscles from cooling and tensing while inactive.

leglet *see pantalettes*

Leg warmers
Knitted acrylic yarn
Scotland/Macau/Hong Kong, *c.*1983
V&A: Misc.355(3,4)–1983

leotard a close-fitting legless garment, usually with sleeves, worn mainly for gymnastics or ballet, later also as a fashion garment.
dates late 19th century in theatrical use; earliest printed mention 1920 (OED).
derivation from Jules Léotard (died 1870), celebrity trapeze artist. Léotard, the inspiration of George Leybourn's song about 'the daring young man on the flying trapeze', was the inventor of the trapeze act as we know it, as well as the close-fitting garment on which the modern leotard is based.

Leotard
Cotton
British, *c.*1959
V&A: Misc.267–1981

liberty bodice a child's close-fitting front-fastening underbodice of knitted fabric strengthened with cotton tape, designed mainly by Fred Cox, a director of the corsetry firm R. & W.H. Symington and Co. of Market Harborough. The Liberty bodice was so successful that it was copied by other firms, and also made in adult sizes. A special buttonless wrapover design for babies was introduced by Symingtons in 1920. *Also called* **utility bodice**
dates 1908 to about 1960.
derivation implies 'liberty from stays'.

Symington's Ltd,
liberty bodice for a baby
Knitted fabric
British, 1925–30
V&A: Misc.118(1)–1984

Bottom
Kosybak brand,
Utility Scheme, liberty
bodice for a girl
Knitted fabric
British, 1942–52
V&A: Misc.587–1985

livery originally clothing of a particular colour or combination of colours, often including a recognisable badge or device, worn by servants, family members or employees to show allegiance to an individual or company. From the 18th century, livery in the formal sense was principally worn by male servants such as pageboys and footmen.
dates from the Middle Ages onward. Millions of teenagers currently experience it in the modern practice of employers such as supermarkets issuing staff with overalls in the company colours.
derivation ultimately from Latin *liberare*, 'to liberate, hand over' in the sense of handing out clothing to servants.

Pageboy's livery jacket
Wool
British, 1899
V&A: MoC

loafer™ a type of shoe resembling a *moccasin* but with a separately attached sole.
dates 1930s onward, though not familiar in Britain until the 1950s.
derivation originally a brand name: the loafer is casual wear associated with the verb *to loaf*, 'to be idle'.

long barrow *see barracoat*

long bib a piece of rectangular cloth worn over a baby's swaddling bands, running from beneath the chin to the feet, and pinned in place.
dates 16th century to 18th century.
derivation descriptive.

long clothes, long clothes layette the long garments worn by babies after swaddling went out of use. See *Appendix 1*

long johns (informal) long-legged underpants, usually of warm fabric, for men and boys; sometimes also used to describe long-legged combinations.
dates 1850s onward as a style, but apparently only called 'long johns' from the 1940s.
derivation uncertain. Said to be named after American boxer John L. Sullivan (1858–1918), who wore a similar garment in the ring, and was one of the best known fighters of the 1880s.

long stay (part of swaddling) *see stayband*

Norvic brand, loafers
Leather
British, 1945–50
V&A: Misc.308&A–1979

Opposite
Long johns
Knitted wool fabric
British, *c*.1850
V&A: Misc.4–1961 (part)

Long bib
Linen
British, *c*.1700
V&A: Misc.323(6)–1984

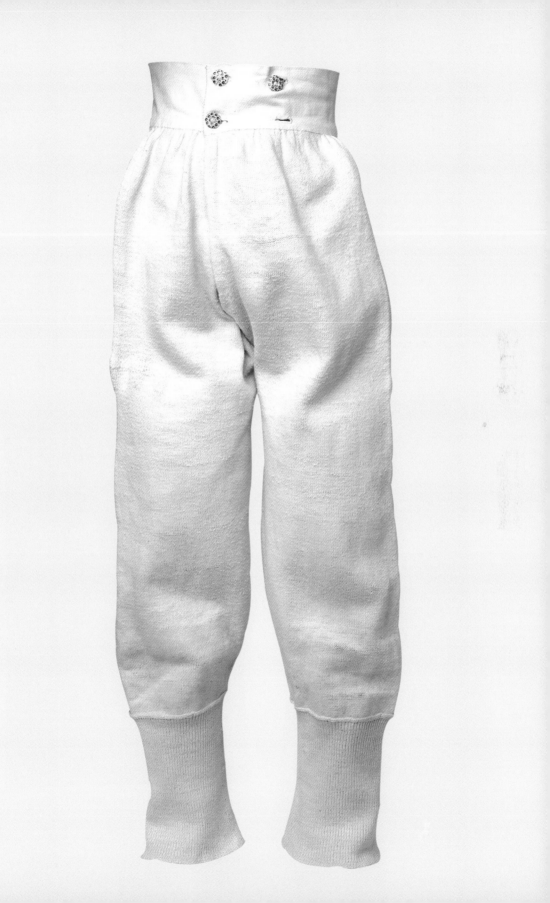

loons, loon trousers, loon pants

casual trousers flared exaggeratedly wide
in the lower leg.

dates about 1970–75.

derivation the OED derives the name of this
garment from the verb *to loon*, 'spend time in a
pleasurable way', but some contemporary usage
implied that it was either an abbreviation
for **pantaloons** or *loon* in the sense of 'loony,
mad person' (not necessarily an unfavourable
comment in the 1970s); another theory is that
the word is short for *balloon pants*.

Falmers brand, loons
Cotton
British, *c*.1971
V&A: Misc.753–1986

lumber jacket a short, long-sleeved jacket

of warm fabric or knitted wool, usually zip-
fastening, sometimes with buckles and tabs at
the sides.

date 1930s to present day.

derivation originally worn by those working in
the North American lumber (timber) industry.

lumber suit *see snow suit*

Patons & Baldwins Ltd,
knitting pattern for
lumber jackets
Printed paper
British, 1955–60
V&A: Misc.61(39)–1990

mM

mac, mack, macintosh, mackintosh

mac, mack, **macintosh**, **mackintosh** a waterproof coat. The idea was revolutionary when introduced, and eminently suitable for childrenswear, but the problem with the rubberized fabric of the early examples was evidently the smell. By the 1880s various manufacturers were advertising that their products contained no India rubber, and therefore no smell, although the firm of J. Mandelburg & Co. warned that '… in wear SUCH goods are liable to become more offensive than ever, the substance used having a tendency to turn sour and become putrid; whereas, in marked contrast, a Mandelburg Garment is guaranteed PERMANENTLY free from smell, and will wear sweet to the last thread' (advertisement, *Myra's Journal*, 1 December 1890). The garment went on to become a staple in children's wardrobes, and included in school uniform lists. Selfridges offered bargains in children's waterproof capes and coats from the 1920s. *Also called* **raincoat**, **waterproof**

pacamac™ 20th-century brand-named plastic waterproof, so light in weight that it could be easily rolled up and carried in case of rain.

dates 1830s onward.

derivation from the surname of Charles Mackintosh (1766–1843), inventor of a waterproof fabric (layers of fabric combined with rubber dissolved in naphtha) which he patented on 17 June 1823.

man-o'-war suit *see* *sailor suit*

manteau *another name for* *coat*

Selfridges advertisement
for a mackintosh
Printed paper
British, 1931
V&A: MoC

Fleecy Lined Macs for the KIDDIES

10 D.E. 548.—Your little boy or girl will be dry and warm in one of these fleecy lined leatherette macintoshes, with sou'wester to match. The raglan style leaves room for another coat underneath, the lining is soft and fleecy. The sizes, 21, 24, and 27 ins., fit children from 2 to 6 years old, and the colours are Saxe, Almond, Tan, Red or Black. British made. SPECIAL PRICE, the set

5/11

Postage 6d. extra.
Please state second choice of colour.
*(Selfridge's
Bargain
Basement,
Aisle 17B)*

mantle 1 a wrap or garment like a long sleeveless waistcoat for a baby. In the 19th century the word was sometimes used as a synonym for *carrying cape*. **2** an outer garment, see *cloak*, *coat*.

dates 16th century to 19th century. The OED quotes T. Dyche and W. Pardon, *A new general English dictionary* of 1735: '*Mantle* … the upper-most Garment that Nurses wrap up young infants in before they coat 'em.'

derivation of debated origin, probably from post-classical Latin *mantellum*.

mantua see *gown*

mary jane, **Mary Jane** a low-heeled shoe with an instep strap, more commonly called 'strap shoe' in Britain.

dates early 20th century onward.

derivation an archetypal girl's name for an archetypal girl's shoe (the phrase was not used for strap shoes worn by young boys).

Kiddie Komfort brand,
mary jane shoes
Leather
British, 1930–39
V&A: Misc.214(1,2)–1986

matinée coat, matinée jacket

originally an adult garment, later a baby's loose-fitting long-sleeved knitted jacket with fastenings on the yoke or bodice only. The form **matinée** alone was a less common usage: 'All readers who decide to make this Robe, Cap, and Matinée cannot fail to be delighted with its delicate, lacy charm' (*Woman's Magazine*, 1932, quoted in *Some Things for the Children*).

dates 1920s onward.

derivation French *matin*, 'morning', the original adult garment being worn in the morning.

maxi, maxi dress *see dress*

Matinée coat
Crocheted wool
British, *c*.1939
V&A: Misc.553–1991

middy, middy blouse, middy dress, middy suit

a loose-fitting slip-on blouse, often with sailor collar. The dress format also had a middy bodice like the blouse. The suit had a short button-through jacket (in line with midshipman's uniform of the period).

dates 1890 onward.

derivation from *midshipman*, a naval officer whose position was originally in the middle of the ship.

mini, mini dress *see dress*

Matinée coat
Knitted wool
British, *c*.1944
V&A: Misc.210–1985

mitten, **mitt 1** a glove with half-length fingers. **2** a full-length fingerless glove, usually with a thumb, but sometimes without, especially for babies. Mittens on a string or ribbon round a young child's neck date back to at least the early 17th century, as shown by Anne Buck in illustration 113 of *Clothes and the Child* (the painting is of the Tasburgh family in about 1615).

infantee a thumbless mitten for a baby, the word modelled on *bootee, muffatee,* etc. (instructions included in the Scotch Wool Shop knitting booklet *What to Knit for Baby,* published by Fleming, Reid & Co. Ltd, *c*.1930).

scratch mitten a mitten for babies and small children to prevent them scratching their faces, notably at night or when a rash or other skin problem has occurred.

dates 1287–8 (OED) onward. '… long cotton or thread mitts, without fingers, tied round the arm high above the elbow', Charlotte Papendiek on the clothing of her eleven-month-old daughter, in 1783 (Pollock).

derivation from French *mitaine.*

mob cap (frequently misspelt as 'mop cap') a round, frilled fabric cap with a bouffant crown, for indoor wear, usually made from a piece of circular fabric gathered near the edge to form a face-framing frill, or gathered into a band with a frill added. Originally high fashion, but later associated with female servants, the mob cap was also considered a picturesque revival for children in the late 19th century, especially as part of a Kate Greenaway outfit or other historicizing style of dress. A version called 'Cherry Ripe' (clearly based on the one worn in Millais' 1879 painting of the same name) and costing ten shillings and sixpence was the central feature of an advertisement for children's hats by the clothing firm Hilder & Godbold in *Myra's Journal*, 1 June 1881.

dates 18th century to early 20th century.

derivation *mob*, 'woman, wench', possibly from the name Mab.

Mob cap for a doll
Muslin with ribbon
British, *c*.1740
V&A: Misc.271–1981

Mitten   *Bottom*
Knitted and   Mitten
embroidered wool   Knitted thread
British, *c*.1938   Irish 1886–90
V&A: Misc.248(1,2)–1984   V&A: Misc.123(1,2)–1983

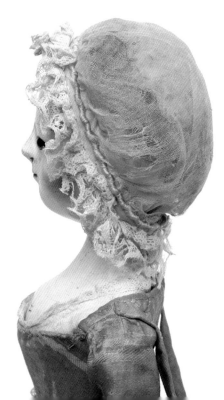

moccasin a type of soft shoe with the sole extending vertically up the foot, and connected by a flap of fabric across the top.

dates in childrenswear, late 19th century onward.

derivation a native American shoe, with similar names in various tribal languages, e.g. *mockasin, mowhcasun* (Powhatan).

Moccasins
Suede with beads and
rabbit fur
Canadian, *c.*1982
V&A: Misc.858(1,2)–1991

Below
Minnetonka
brand moccasins
Leather with bead trim
USA, 1972
V&A: Misc.502(1,2)–1985

Montem costume the increasingly fanciful outfits worn by the boys of Eton College for their triennial Montem procession and celebrations. The writer Maria Edgeworth's 1799 account describes some of the costumes 'made as usual, very handsomely, by Mrs. Snow, milliner, of Windsor'; even Mr Islip, who is stated to be in mourning, wearing 'a scarf, helmet, black velvet and white satin'. An article in *The Illustrated London News* (1 June 1844) shows engravings of Montem costumes for that year which include a Hungarian Hussar, a Crusader, a Spanish peasant and Sir Walter Raleigh, and is untiring in its descriptions of crimson satin, blue leather buskins and gold braid and lace.

dates from at least 1561 until the last Montem procession was held in 1847, after which the custom was suppressed.

derivation the procession was described as being *ad montem*, 'to the hill or mound' in Latin, and referred to Salt Hill, also known as Montem Mound, in Slough, Berkshire. The boys would exact a gratuity called *salt* from all who passed by, sometimes collecting as much as £1,000, to support the captain of the school in his university studies.

Montem costume illustrations,
Illustrated London News
Printed paper
British, 1844
V&A: MoC

mourning, **half mourning** the
garments worn for a set period of time to mark
sorrow at the death of a relative or friend.
While adults and older children wore black for
mourning, young children's mourning garments
were often white, particularly for the death
of another child. Half mourning colours were
shades of grey and purple, or white with black.
dates black clothing from the 14th century
onward.
derivation of uncertain origin, possibly from
Old English *bemurnan, bimurnan*.

muckinder, **muckender**,
muckinger, **muckiter**, **mockateer**
(many similar variations) a large handkerchief,
resembling a hand towel, worn hanging from
the waist by young children.
dates from at least 16th century to 18th century.
derivation origin obscure, but probably from the
Catalan verb *mocarse*, 'blow one's nose', related
to French *mouchoir*, 'handkerchief'.

Muckinder, 1587
From *Children on Brasses*
by John Page Phillips
Printed paper
(London, 1970)

muff a cylinder of fabric, fur or feathers into
which the hands can be tucked to keep them
warm; also used to carry small items such as a
purse, handkerchief or book, particularly if the
ends are filled in with fabric cuffs; sometimes
worn hanging from a 'muff string' around the
neck.
dates 1550s to present day.
derivation from Dutch *mof* or German *muff*.

Muff
Afghan fur
French, 1920–29
V&A: B.150–1999

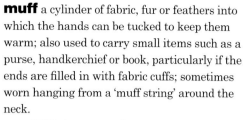

muffatee, **muffetee** 1 a wrist warmer, like a small muff, worn in pairs. **2** a type of *mitten*.

dates 18th and 19th centuries. 'I've only got the muffatees for Papa' (S. Coolidge, *What Katy Did*, 1872).

derivation diminutive of muff.

muffler *see scarf*

Muffatee
Sheepskin
British, 1902–8
V&A: B.75–1995

mukluk, **muk** a short lightweight boot of soft material; originally worn by native Americans of the Arctic region, and made of e.g. reindeer or seal skin, sometimes lined with fur. Modern European mukluks are more often made from fleece or knitted fabric. *Also called* **kamak**, **kamik**

dates traditional to present day.

derivation) mukluk is of Yupik origin, from *maklak*, 'bearded seal'; kamik is an Inuit word.

mule a backless slipper; later female styles sometimes with an open toe.

dates 1550s onward.

derivation from Middle French *mule*, 'slipper'.

muslin square *see nappy liner*

Mule
Velvet and leather
Turkish, 19th century
V&A: Circ.28–1917

nN oO

nappy, **napkin** (US **diaper**) a garment or cloth covering the lower part of a baby's torso, to absorb and retain faeces and urine.

bapkin probably a conflation of the words 'baby napkin', the brand name for a disposable nappy pad made by The Sanitary Wood Wool Co. (advertisement in *Myra's Journal*, 1 June 1888).

disposable, **disposable nappy** a nappy to be thrown away after a single use. Full-sized disposable nappies, as opposed to the disposable pads such as the bapkin and knapkenette, were available from the 1940s onward.

knapkenette the brand name of disposable nappy pads made by Southall's (advertisement in *Myra's Journal*, 1 July 1890).

reusable, **reusable nappy** a nappy that could be washed and reused, which before the introduction of disposables, had been simply known as 'a nappy' without qualification.

dates napkin was certainly in use by the 1840s, the garment itself had been in use under the name **tailclout** since at least the Middle Ages.

derivation *nap* with the diminutive suffix *-kin* or *-py*, 'a little piece of linen cloth'.

nappy cover *see pilch*

Harringtons brand nappy
Terry towelling
British, 1957
V&A: Misc.747–1992

Disposable nappy
Waterproofed paper
British, c.2002
V&A: MoC

Opposite
Ella's House brand, nappy
Printed hemp cloth
(Queen Elizabeth II's Golden Jubilee commemorative)
Scottish, 2002
V&A: B.8–2003

Norfolk jacket a close-fitting long-sleeved jacket of hardwearing material, with various reinforcing straps of self fabric; worn by boys and men, particularly in the country, and derived from an earlier garment called the Norfolk shirt.

dates at least 1890s onward for boys.

derivation from the English county.

Bertie Stone in a Norfolk
jacket (and his brother
Harold in a Fauntleroy suit),
by W.H. Palmer
Photographic print
British, c.1895
V&A: MoC

occasion wear formal clothing worn for social events and celebrations such as parties, weddings, Bar Mitzvahs, Bat Mitzvahs, First Communions, Confirmations, etc.

dates most characteristic of the 1970s onward, and particularly used in the clothing industry and related media.

derivation descriptive.

orthopaedic garments

orthopaedic garments orthopaedic items are designed to help treat physical deformity in children. An early documented example is the case of Charles, Duke of York, later King Charles I (born 1600). Between 1605 and 1611 he was in the guardianship of Sir Robert and Lady Carey, who took great trouble with his walking and speech difficulties, and ordered orthopaedic boots of leather and brass for him, among other treatments. At a less official level, the V&A Museum of Childhood has a pair of lace-up clogs which were made in the 1920s for a child with weak ankles. *See also **ear cap**.*

oval trousers *see **trousers***

Example of orthopaedic
wear: clogs
Leather and wood
British, *c.*1925
V&A: MoC

Bottom
Norvic Kiltie brand,
oxford shoes
Leather
British, 1949–55
V&A: Misc.260&A–1979

overall 1 a protective garment added as an outer layer to keep the wearer's clothing clean. *Also called **dust cloak**, **dust coat**, **dust gown**, **dust wrap** 2* closed-foot leggings for a baby. **3** (US) dungarees.

dates trousers and leggings were among the earliest forms, from the late 18th century onward; the coat-like garment which is the modern version is recorded from the 1870s onward.

derivation descriptive.

overcoat *see **coat***

oxford, oxford shoe

oxford, **oxford shoe** a type of lace-up shoe with the paired tabs for the lace holes positioned within the body of the shoe; in general less often found in children's shoes than the ***derby***, but a style which has been favoured for school uniform shoes, particularly in private schools.

dates early 19th century onward.

derivation from the city and university of Oxford.

Bentalls' brand, overall
Cotton
British, *c.*1935
V&A: Misc.88–1984

pP qQ

pageboy suit, pageboy's suit, page's suit

clothing worn by a boy (sometimes designated ring-bearer) attendant upon the bride at a wedding. Like brides and bridesmaids, pages originally wore clothing which generally reflected the fashion of the day, but when the white wedding became the established form in the 19th century, their clothing became more fanciful. Kate Greenaway styles, sailor suits and Scotch suits have probably had the greatest popularity, but historical styles had a particular vogue in the 1880s and '90s.

dates mid-17th century onward.
derivation French *page*, of obscure origin.

pajamas see *pyjamas*

palazzo pants see *trousers*

paletot

used to describe a variety of outdoor garments, but in children's clothing usually a short or three-quarter length loose-fitting outdoor coat without a waist seam.

dates 1800s–1890s.
derivation French *paletot*.

palm see *bearing cloth*

Pageboy's suit (wedding)
Satin with lace
British, 1894
V&A: Misc.262(1,2)–1983

Engraving of a paletot,
Myra's Journal of Dress and Fashion
Printed paper
British, 1889
V&A: MoC

panama, **panama hat** a hat of
pale plaited straw with a curving brim, in
childrenswear particularly associated with
girls' school uniform, but sometimes worn
as a summer hat.

dates in original form, a hat of plaited palm
leaves; the straw equivalent appears to have
been available since at least the 1830s. Later
examples sometimes bore the words 'Genuine
Panama' on the inside.

derivation from Panama in Central America.

Panama hat
Straw with velveteen
British, 1925–30
V&A: B.655–1993

pantalettes long-legged drawers worn
beneath a dress. Some authorities, notably
James Laver, equate *pantalette* with **leglet**,
a cheaper and more easily maintained form,
a frilled tube of fabric tied on at each knee.

*Also called **trousers**, **trowsers***

dates 1810s to 1850, surviving in younger
children's clothes into the 1860s.

derivation as in *pantaloons*.

Pantalettes
Cambric
British, *c*.1800
V&A: T.211–1934

pantaloons 1 long, close-fitting trousers. Breeches were still considered by many the more correct form of trousers for boys until well on into the 19th century. In 1800 Scrope Berdmore Davies's tailor billed him four shillings and sixpence for 'making panterlunes In to breeches and [with] Coverd buttons' to wear at Eton because he was a Colleger (holding a King's Scholarship) and not allowed to wear trousers (T.A.J. Burnett, *The Rise and Fall of a Regency Dandy*). **2** sometimes used to describe long straight trousers worn under a dress, but these were more typically referred to as *pantalettes* or *trowsers*.
dates 1 about 1795–1815, then superseded by the looser fitting ***trousers***. **2** 1810s–50s, superseded by ***drawers***.
derivation from the character Pantaloon in Venetian drama, ultimately from San Pantal(e)one, the patron saint of the city.

pants 1 *see knickers* **2** *see trousers*

pantyhose *see tights*

paper dress *see dress*

Pantaloons
Cotton
British, 1800–1815
V&A: Misc.66(2)–1988

parasol, **sunshade** a metal frame on a stem, covered with fabric, to shield the user's head and face from the sun.
dates as a fashion, approximately 1800–1920, but continuing in the form of the Japanese paper sunshade in the 1920s and '30s, with a minor revival as a novelty item in the 1970s, and as an accessory on prams and baby carriages to the present day.
derivation from Italian *parasole*, 'for [protection against] the sun', via French.

Farge of Paris, parasol
Silk and metal
with ivory handle
French, 1840–60
V&A: B.203–1996

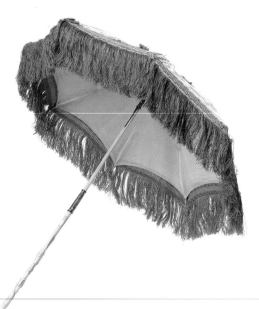

parka a long-sleeved waterproof jacket, usually with a fur-trimmed hood, originally with a longer bifurcated hem at the back (sometimes called a **fishtail parka**).
snorkel, **snorkel coat**, **snorkel jacket**, **snorkel parka** a waterproof jacket with long sleeves, and a fur-trimmed hood which projected forward around the face when pulled up over the head, the coat itself resembling a short parka but sometimes quilted. Parkas and snorkel jackets were banned by some schools because of the potential danger of the hood obscuring a child's vision crossing the road. The hoods also had considerable play or nuisance value (putting hoods together and staring, using straps to grab opponent or attach to bus seat, wearing hood up and breathing out to emulate steam train, etc.).

dates probably first available in Britain as army surplus in the 1960s, and certainly made for civilian fashion from at least the 1970s ('anoraks, duffels and snorkels', *Children's Clothing International*, March 1981).
derivation *parka* is an Inuit word for a garment made from animal skins. The cloth version was available from at least the 1930s in the USA. The post-war fashion appears to derive from a USAF waterproof fabric garment of 1947. The usage of the word *snorkel* arose from a perceived resemblance between the hood encircling the face and the mask worn with a snorkel in underwater swimming.

party dress, **party frock**, **party clothes** *see evening dress*

Parka
Nylon with fur fabric
British, 1976
V&A: Misc.588–1992

patten a protective wooden sole with a toecap or instep strap to keep it on the foot, sometimes also raised on a metal ring or block, and worn by girls and women over shoes to keep their feet (and footwear) out of mud, snow, puddles, etc.

dates around 1390–1837; Mrs Gaskell cites their use in *Cranford* (set in the early 1840s) to indicate an unfashionable way of life, 'The inhabitants of Cranford kept early hours and clattered home in their pattens'.

derivation from French *patin*, 'clog', possibly from *patte*, 'paw'.

pea coat, **pea jacket** *see reefer jacket*

Pattens
Leather, wood and metal
British, 1780–1820
V&A: B.76(1,2)–1997

pedal pushers short trousers for women or girls, fairly close-fitting and usually either lightly gathered into a cuff at the knee or reaching to just below the knee.

dates 1944 onward in the USA.

derivation said to be derived from jeans or trousers rolled up for cycling.

pelerine *see cape*

Pedal pushers
Cotton
USA, 1960–65
V&A: B.129(2)–1999

pelisse 1 originally a cloak with an additional short cape; later a caped coat with sleeves. **2** another name for a baby's *carrying cape*.

dates 18th and 19th centuries: '..we make our own clothes, our frocks, and pelisses, and everything' (Charlotte Brontë, *Jane Eyre*, 1847).

derivation from Latin *pellicia*, 'fur coat or other garment', via French, *pelice*, *pellicle*, 'fur (or fur-lined) robe'.

pelisse-robe a coat-like dress based on the pelisse, with full wrist-length sleeves, and fastening the length of the front with bows or other ornaments.

dates 1820s–50s.

derivation as *pelisse* above.

Pelisse robe
Printed cotton
British, *c.*1840
V&A: Misc.9(22A)–1977

peplum a length of fabric hanging below the waist of a girl's or woman's jacket or dress. In modern usage, a pendant frill attached at the waist.

dates 1860s onward. 'It's never too soon to be fashion conscious. She'll love wearing this durable grey flannel suit. The tailored jacket has the newest flared peplum …' (Selfridges advertisement for a girl's suit in the *Daily Express*, 9 May 1949).

derivation from Greek *peplos*, a garment for the upper body, falling in loose folds from the shoulders.

Peter Pan collar *see collar*

Peplum on a dress
Rayon blend
German, *c.*1930
V&A: B.51–2004

petticoat 1 an undergarment worn beneath a skirt, and resembling one (although sometimes with a bodice added) but not intended to be visible. Petticoats provided shape to the skirt, and were sometimes worn in multiple layers, particularly before the use of the crinoline and bustle. In children's clothing, petticoats were held to be particularly important in preventing them from catching cold, but some clothes reformers and their followers deplored petticoats as unnecessary if the rest of the undergarments were correctly designed and made from suitable fabrics. *Also called* **slip**, **underskirt**. **2** a decorative underskirt intended to be visible. Older girls and women in the 18th century, for example, would wear petticoats of quilted coloured fabric with their open-fronted gowns. A later variation was the coloured petticoat sometimes worn by younger girls beneath a dress of sheer white fabric to produce a pastel effect, or beneath a white cutwork frock to give a decorative effect. **can-can petticoat** a waist petticoat resembling the skirts of can-can dancers, of exaggeratedly full shape, made up of numerous layers of stiff net, popular in the 1950s and early 1960s.

dates 1 16th century onward **2** from the 16th century, in and out of fashion until the 1910s.

derivation *petty*, 'small' + coat (originally referring to a garment more like a waistcoat).

petticoat bodice *see camisole*

picture dress, **picture frock**, **picture gown** a romanticized version of women's and girls' historic dress, often with tiers of frills in the skirt and worn with a large hat; often chosen for bridesmaids' dresses and for representing the 19th century in fancy dress costume.

dates 1880s onward, but for children mainly 1920s and '30s.

derivation 'like clothing in a picture' (copied from or inspired by clothing worn in Old Master portraits); popular usage was possibly augmented by *the pictures*, 'the cinema', a precursor of which was known as 'living pictures'.

Petticoat
Cotton
British, *c*.1840
V&A: Misc.9(5)–1977

Below left
Can-can petticoat
Nylon, net and nylon lace
British, 1950–59
V&A: Misc.229–1979

Opposite
Girl wearing a picture dress at the Lord Mayor of London's Children's Ball, by Bassano
Photographic print
British, 1936
V&A: B.222(20)–1996

pilch, **pilcher** a cover for a baby's nappy, either in the form of a triangular wrap or a garment resembling a pair of knickers. They were sometimes reinforced, presumably to contain moisture better. In 1768, the year of her second son's birth, Lady Shelburne bought 'double pilches'. Waterproof versions made of 'mackintosh fabric' became available after it was patented in 1823. 'Waterproof pilches, such as the "Baby's Napkin Protector" should on no account be used … by preventing the escape of heat and moisture from the body [they] keep it … in a state of perpetual poultice', warned Ada S. Ballin in *The Science of Dress* (1885). They were superseded by **waterproof pants** made of synthetic fabrics and eventually plastic.
Also called **nappy cover**
dates from the 17th century onward, and still in use in the Second World War (although Alice Guppy comments in *Children's Clothes 1939–1970* that even in the childrenswear trade few knew the meaning of the word by 1943); *pilcher* is now a mainly Australian and New Zealand term.
derivation originally an outer garment made of animal skin, from non-classical Latin *pellicia*, 'furry'.

Pilch
Linen
British, c.1909
V&A: Misc.377(1)–1982

pin, **pincushion** before safety pins were widely available, ordinary pins were often used as a means of fastening clothes and other textiles together, and persisted in use in baby clothes in particular because they allowed for easy adjustment of garments and swaddling on a growing infant. Pins were originally made by hand, and as they were quite expensive, careful householders would keep them safe. Fabric pincushions were in general household use from at least the 16th century, and were also popular as courting and wedding presents or New Year's gifts. *See also* **safety pin**
layette pincushions once customary presents for a new mother, and most popular between about 1770 and 1890. They were usually given after the baby had arrived, as there was a superstitious belief that they could increase the pain felt by the mother during birth: 'For every pin a pain' and 'More pins, more pain'. And at a time when many problems could arise during childbirth, some felt that it was taking too much for granted to give such items beforehand.
dates 13th century onward.
derivation from Latin *pinna*, 'point', 'tip'.

Pincushion
Silk
British, 1862
V&A: Misc.142–1985

Pincushion
Cotton
British, 1830–50
V&A: Misc.238–1988

Bottom
Pincushion
Painted velvet
British, 1838
V&A: Misc.93–1985

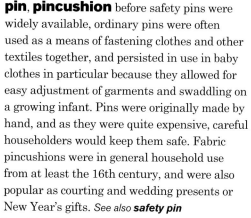

pinafore, **pincloth**, **pinner** informally
pinnie, **pinny** a protective garment worn
to keep the clothes clean, originally a type of
apron pinned to the clothes at the front, later
a collarless, sleeveless overall, fastening at
the back. Like bibs, pinafores could also be
almost purely decorative, notably when made
of lace, net or broderie anglaise. This usage has
survived in clothes for younger girls.

pinafore dress (US *jumper*) a sleeveless
collarless dress to wear over a blouse or jumper.
Its modern popularity probably derives at
least in part from the *gymslip*. *Weldon's Home
Dressmaker No 331, School Outfits & Every
Day Wear* suggests that the gymslip is 'useful
for home or school wear'.

pinafore suit a young boy's garment, perhaps
originally like a pinafore dress but bifurcated at
the hem. Eve Garnett describes her character
Anthony Perkins as wearing one in *The Family
from One End Street* (1937) and draws it as
shorts with shoulder straps.

dates in the sense of a protective garment, from
the late 18th century; by the early years of the
20th century worn only by younger children,
although still in general use in some parts of
continental Europe. From being one of the
most characteristic garments of childhood, the
pinafore became largely unnecessary even for
younger children after the Second World War,
with improvements in detergents and washable
fabrics, and the greater availability of washing
machines. One of the last traces of its survival
is the *tabard*, still in use for art and dressing-up
activities for younger children.

derivation from the action of its original putting
on (pin afore = pin on in front), *pincloth* and
pinner being similarly formed.

pink for a girl *see gender indicators*

pinner *see pinafore*

pinnie, **pinny** *see pinafore*

pinning blanket *see barracoat*

Pinafore for a girl
Cotton
British, *c*.1840
V&A: Misc.9(18)–1977

Pinafore for a boy
Cotton
British, *c*.1918
V&A: Misc.211–1979

Laura Ashley,
pinafore dress
Printed cotton
British, 1985
V&A: B.128–1993

pixie boot a short boot, often of suede or similar leather, with a pointed toe and the top folded over in a pointed or bifurcated cuff.
dates 1980s onward.
derivation from the footwear of pixies as illustrated in children's books.

pixie hood, also **pixie cap**, **pixie hat**
a cap or attached hood with a pointed tip.
dates pixie cap is known from the 1820s but is most typically found in connection with children's clothing from about 1930 onward.
derivation from the typical headgear of pixies as illustrated in children's books.

pixie suit see **snowsuit**

play slacks see **dungarees**

Utility Scheme
pixie hood
Knitted wool
British, 1942–52
V&A: Misc.590–1985

plimsoll a flat canvas shoe with textured sole (originally rubber, later a synthetic substitute) with either lace-up (generally oxford type) fastening or in slip-on style with an elasticated panel at the front. *Also called* **gym shoe**, **rubber** (US **sneaker**)
dates this application of the name from 1876 onward.
derivation Samuel Plimsoll (1824–98) invented the Plimsoll line to show how deeply in the water a ship might safely sit when loading; the line between the sole and the canvas upper of the shoe evidently recalled this, and indicated the level below which the shoe was waterproof.

plus twos, **plus fours** see **knickerbockers**

Plimsolls
Canvas with rubber composition
British, 1950–59
V&A: Misc.324&A–1979

pocket formerly a separate fabric bag (sometimes worn in pairs) tied round the waist beneath the skirt and reached by means of a placket or slit in the front of the skirt. 'Lucy Locket lost her pocket' (traditional rhyme).
dates up to about 1850.
derivation Anglo-Norman *poket(e)*, *pochete*, 'small bag'.

pocket handkerchief *see handkerchief*

poke bonnet, **poking bonnet** *see bonnet*

Pockets for a doll
Embroidered linen
British, 1780–1800
V&A: Misc.61(7)–1964

polonaise a separate, and shorter, upper part of a dress, usually in the form of a light coat or bodice and skirt, either caught up in front and behind, or open at the skirt front and caught up behind. In girl's clothing, the appearance of a polonaise upper part of a dress is due to the influence of the **Kate Greenaway** styles.
dates 1770s–80s, and again in the 1870s. 'Little Girl's Polonaise' (dress pattern advertised in *Myra's Journal*, 1 December 1879).
derivation French *polonaise*, 'Polish', believed to have been based on the clothing of Polish women.

pompon *see topknot*

poncho an unfitted throw-over cape, usually a lozenge-shaped or rectangular piece of woven or knitted fabric with a central hole for the neck.

dates traditional costume in Latin American cultures. Popular as a fashion item around 1964 to 1974, probably from the one worn by Clint Eastwood's character The Man With No Name in the 1964 film *A Fistful of Dollars*. Some ponchos are still marketed as 'Clint Eastwood ponchos'. The poncho was revived in 2004, often in a shorter length than the original, and in pastel colours was particularly popular with sub-teen girls. The word *poncho* has also come to be less accurately applied to other garments such as the *serape*, a wrap.

derivation American Spanish *poncho*, of debated origin.

pop sock *see* **sock**

pram set a set of knitted garments for a baby to wear in its pram, usually consisting of coat, hat or bonnet, and mittens, sometimes including bootees or leggings.

dates early 20th century onward.

derivation pram from the word *perambulator* (baby carriage), literally 'someone who walks about' from the Latin verb *perambulare*.

Opposite
Poncho
Crocheted wool
British, *c*.1972
V&A: Misc.535–1985

Glenroyal brand,
pram set
Knitted wool
British 1930–39
V&A: Misc.689(1–3)–1986

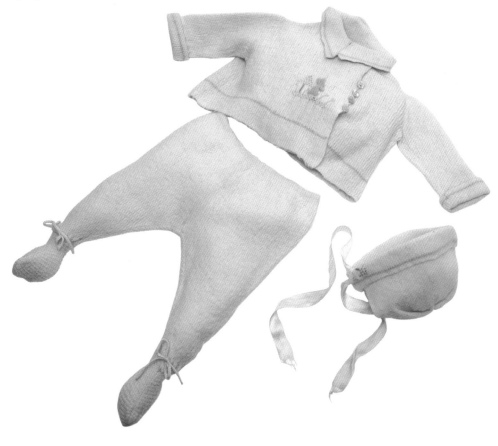

princess coat, **princess dress**, **princess petticoat** one without a waist seam between the bodice and skirt, but usually shaped at the front by two full-length vertical seams curving down over the chest. The absence of a seam encircling the waist made such clothing considered particularly suitable for children, since less pressure was exerted on the internal organs, and the garment stayed in position better in those whose waists were not well defined. 'Little Girl's Princess Dress' heads the list of children's dress patterns available from *Myra's Dress & Pattern Depot* in December 1879 (advertisement, *Myra's Journal*, 1 December 1879). *Also called*

gabrielle dress

dates 1870s onward for children. 'A pretty Gabrielle dress, of a soft, warm shade of brown' (L.M. Alcott, *Eight Cousins*, 1875).

derivation *princess* from Alexandra, Princess of Wales.

pudding, **black pudding** a head protection for a very young child learning to walk. The basic form was a padded tube of fabric tied around the head just above the ears, sometimes with additional flaps tied together at the crown of the head. Most puddings were for practical purposes only, and many were home made, but they could also be formal and decorative. In 1766 Lady Shelburne's diary records that her son Lord Fitzmaurice on his first birthday wore a muslin frock over a rose-coloured damask coat, and 'a rose collour pudding with black & white feathers in it'.

dates 17th century to about 1800.

derivation generally believed to be from French *boudin*, 'black pudding', from its sausage-like form, though the OED has an interesting link to regional German *puddel*, 'a small person, small fat child, esp. a child just beginning to walk'.

Pudding
Cotton with ribbon
British, 1775–1800
V&A: B.81–1995

pullover a knitted tunic, originally 'pull-over sweater'. More or less synonymous with jersey, jumper, sweater.
dates 1920s onward.
derivation descriptive, from the action of putting it on over the head.

Golden Eagle knitting
pattern for pullovers
Printed paper
British, 1950–55
V&A: Misc.534(13)–1986

pump a type of flat shoe; in modern usage also a type of athletics shoe.
dates 1550s onward.
derivation unknown.

Pump
Satin
British, c.1850
V&A: T.546&A–1913

pyjamas, **pajamas** a jacket or tunic and trousers for wearing in bed (and formerly also as underwear), adapted from Asian garments. "'Mercy on us, these things are like the night-drawers Jamie wears! You don't mean to say you want Rose to come out in this costume?' … "I do mean it, and I'm sure my sensible aunt will consent when she understands that these pajamas are for underwear'" (L.M. Alcott, *Eight Cousins*, 1875).

baby doll pyjamas, **baby dolls** a short full nightdress over matching knickers.

pajamarette brand name for a type of pyjamas marketed by Pasolds.

dates pyjamas from around 1800 (OED); baby doll pyjamas available in Britain for children from the early 1960s.

derivation pyjama from Persian and Urdu *pae/pay jamah*, 'leg garment'; baby doll pyjamas probably from the 1956 film *Baby Doll*, in which a character of the same name poses holding a very short nightdress against herself.

quartered cap see *cap*

Pyjamas
Cotton
European, 1930–39
V&A: Misc.550(1–2)–1986

rR

ra-ra skirt, **rah-rah skirt** a short skirt with layered frills; also **ra-ra** or **rah-rah dress**, one with a skirt similarly constructed.
dates 1980s.
derivation from *rah-rah,* US expression associated with cheering on collegiate sports teams, and in particular *rah-rah girl,* a cheerleader who characteristically wore a very short skirt.

C&A, ra-ra skirt
with blouse
Cotton
British, *c.*1979
V&A: Misc.491(1,2)–1985

receiver a blanket used to receive a newly delivered baby.
dates approximately 1680s–1900.
derivation descriptive.

reefer, reefer jacket, reefer coat

a short double-breasted jacket or coat, usually
of thick woollen fabric, although reefers for
children were sometimes knitted.

Also called **pea coat**, **pea jacket**

dates 1870s onward.

derivation as worn by sailors, some of whom were
known as reefers.

Illustration of reefer
jackets, *The Royal Navy
of England and the Story
of the Sailor Suit*
Printed paper
British, c.1895–1905
V&A: B.143–1995

reins

reins a harness with straps and/or a leash,
applied to young children to keep them under
control and help prevent them from falling.

dates around 1900 onward, but see also *leading
string*, their precursor

derivation from Latin *retinere*, 'retain'; analogous
with the reins used to restrain and guide
horses and other animals. The V&A Museum
of Childhood collection includes an early set
decorated with a scene of horse racing and the
words 'Race for the Derby'.

Reins
Leather with metal
British, 1930
V&A: Misc.557–1991

riding hood a hood, as in the story of *Little Red Riding Hood*, which inspired a fashion in cloaks for little girls; sometimes a hood with a cloak attached.
dates 1450s to about 1880.
derivation descriptive.

ring-bearer *see **pageboy suit***

robe 1 *see **gown** **2** short for bathrobe, see **dressing gown***

robe blanket *see **barracoat***

Girl wearing a Red
Riding Hood cloak,
by Sydney Victor White
Photographic print
British, c.1880
V&A: MoC

robings the paired edgings which ran, often without a break, from the back of the neck of a gown, across the shoulders, and down the full length of the front of the garment to the hem. They were very much a feature of the long white baby gowns of the 19th century. At first they turned inward, to give the effect of another garment worn over the gown, as in contemporary women's fashions, but then began to be stitched on down the middle, giving a double frill effect, and finally, in about 1835, were attached to the gown along their inner edges and turned outward, in which format they continued for the rest of the century.
dates originally 18th century; in baby clothes, about 1810–1900.
derivation from French *robe*, 'robe or gown'.

roller *see **binder***

roll-on *see **corset***

SYDNEY VICTOR WHITE. MAIDENHEAD.
ERNEST E. WHITE.
Enquiries about this Photograph to be addressed to Reading.

romper, rompers, romper suit

originally a one-piece garment like a combination of a short dress and baggy knickers; later available in two pieces, like a younger child's version of a **buster suit**. *Elizabeth Craig's Needlecraft* (1947) talks of both one- and two-piece rompers as a matter of course, and divides the one-piece garments further into tailored, envelope, and adjustable rompers. *Also called* **creeping overall** *(Wilena Hitching,* Baby Clothing, *1914) and in a drawers-only format as* **crawlers**

dates about 1900 onward.

derivation garment in which a child can *romp*, from French *ramper*, 'to climb'.

rubber *see galosh, plimsoll*

ruff

ruff in the 19th century, a short padded scarf to tie round the neck, 'particularly useful for children' according to *The Workwoman's Guide* (1838). It was evidently thought to resemble a 16th- or 17th-century ruff, the form of which had been revived as a historicizing element in British women's costume in the years around 1800 to 1815.

dates probably 1830s only.

derivation of uncertain origin.

Oxford brand, romper suit
Printed cotton
British, 1925–35
V&A: Misc.654(1)–1986

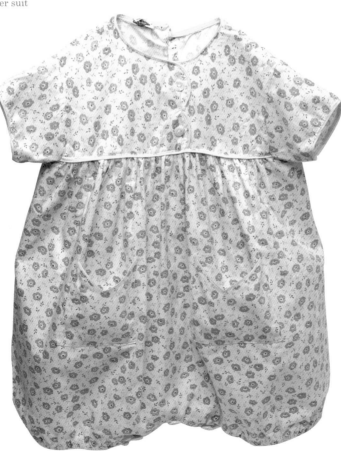

Russian blouse, Russian dress, Russian tunic

1 an asymmetrically fastening garment, loose-fitting, with no waist seam, often with a stand collar and wrist-length gathered sleeves finishing in a cuff.

'Russian' dress
Corduroy with silk lining
British, 1915–20
V&A: Misc.595–1985

Russian suit a suit with a Russian tunic, as above, instead of a jacket.

2 the earlier version, less well known, was an edge-to-edge coat, often fur-trimmed and worn with a sash, baggy trousers and calf-length boots.

dates 1 1890s–1920. **2** 1860s.

derivation adapted from Russian dress.

Swears and Wells Ltd,
'Russian' suit
Linen
British, 1908
V&A: T.157&A–1959

saccarine a short loose-fitting garment resembling a rural smock.

dates probably 19th century only. 'They answer well as morning dresses in which children can run about, and work in the garden, with less danger of tearing or dirtying their under clothes' (*The Workwoman's Guide*, 1838).

derivation unknown; possibly a diminutive of sac, sack, or sacque, in the sense of a loose fitting gown (J. Olian, *Children's Fashions 1860–1912 ... from La Mode Illustrée* shows a broadly similar garment called a *sacque* for a one- to three-year-old in 1870).

sack, **sacque 1** *see* **gown 2** (particularly USA) a type of loose-fitting jacket. 'I'm going to walk, after my lessons, so I wish you'd wear your best hat and sack' (L.M. Alcott, *An Old-fashioned Girl*, 1870).

dates 1 18th century. **2** mainly 1850–1900, surviving some way into the 20th century as a baby garment similar to the British matinée coat.

derivation of uncertain origin.

safety pin, **nappy pin** a looped pin with closable ends, for fastening clothing, particularly that of infants.

dates the principle is that of the fibula, a type of brooch in use from ancient times; the OED gives the earliest printed mention of the phrase *safety pin* as 1857, but the pins were not commonly in use until the introduction of the 'Danish Safety Pin' in 1878.

derivation descriptive, as being safer than the previous long-established practice of pinning clothes with straight pins (as used in dressmaking); throughout the greater part of the 18th and 19th centuries physicians and other reformers campaigned against the use of pins, with little success: '... where fastenings are requisite, they should consist of tape, without the dangerous use of pins' (*The New Female Instructor*, 1834).

Safety nappy pins
Metal
British, 1962
V&A: Misc.759(7)–1988 (part)

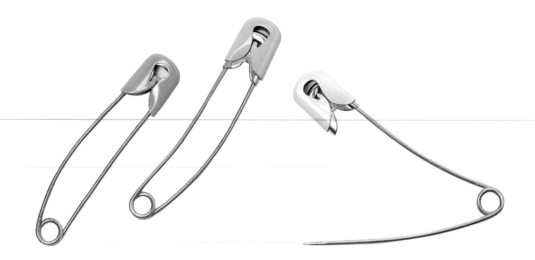

sailor suit a blouse with a square (often detachable) collar, worn with long or short trousers or a skirt or kilted skirt, in a variety of colour combinations: all blue, blue and white, red and white, or all white. Other names included the **Jack tar suit** and the **man-o'-war suit**, the latter claimed by its manufacturers, Redfern of Cowes, to be 'accurately correct to the most minute detail, and … suitable for either sex' (*Myra's Journal*, 1 August 1883). Rowe, one of the leading manufacturers of sailor suits, also offered correct accessories in *The Royal Navy of England and the Story of the Sailor Suit* (*c.*1900) including lanyard and Bo'swain's pipe (whistle), the 'regulation Senet Hat', and the sleeve badges of various naval ranks (although most sailor suits show the anchor and cable of the leading seaman).

dates the first sailor suit for a child is generally acknowledged to be that made for Queen Victoria's eldest son, Prince Albert Edward, to wear on a royal visit to Ireland in 1846. The fashion took a while to become established, but turned into a classic of childrenswear, and was still in use (although tending to be for best) in the 1920s. It survives as a choice for pageboys at weddings. There is an example in the collection at the V&A Museum of Childhood dating from the 1980s.

derivation based on uniform worn by ratings in the Navy.

Sailor suit for a boy
Cotton
British, late 19th century
V&A: Misc.352(1,2)–1979

I.P. Co. brand, the Cecil
Costume sailor suit
Cotton
British, 1920–29
V&A: Misc.265–1978

salopettes dungarees; from the 1970s usually used to describe a similar garment worn beneath a jacket as ski wear.
dates 1970s onward.
derivation from the French word for a child's or workman's overalls.

sand shoe *see beach shoe*

C&A, salopette
and ski jacket
Nylon
British, *c.*1981
V&A: Misc.139(1,2)–1982

sandal 1 footwear consisting of a strap or straps fixed to a sole. **2 dancing sandal** a hard leather version of a ballet shoe; also a strap to fasten this type of shoe. **3 veldtschoen sandal** one constructed by stitching the edge of the upper onto the sole flat rather than turning it under, characteristically with a T-bar strap, but other variations for children included cut-away styles and ankle or instep straps.
dates 1 ancient times to present day. **2** late 18th century to 1930s. **3** 1920s to present day.
derivation from Latin *sandalium*, 'sandal', originally from Greek.

Kiddie Komfort brand,
ankle strap sandals
Leather
British, 1950–59
V&A: Misc.212(1,2)–1986

Norvic brand,
veldtschoen sandals
Leather
English, 1950–59
V&A:Misc.302&A–1979

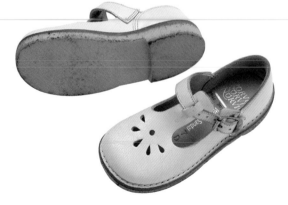

sash a length of decorative fabric, in children's dress usually worn round the waist, but sometimes, especially by boys, diagonally across the chest. In Jane Austen's novel *Mansfield Park* (1814) ten-year-old Fanny Price's cousins 'could not but hold her cheap on finding that she had but two sashes'; this is probably a reflection of the fact that her family really was poor by their standards – a new sash would not be among the more expensive items in a child's wardrobe.

dates 16th century onward.

derivation originally *shash*, an Arabic word for the length of fabric worn as a turban.

Valerie Goad for
Start-Rite, sash
Silk
British, 1982
V&A: Misc.29A–1983

scarf 1 usually a long strip of knitted or woven fabric, to wrap around the neck and/or shoulders, often for warmth. *Also called* **comforter**, **muffler 2** a triangular covering for the head, or a square folded into a triangle. *Also called* **headscarf**, **kerchief**

dates scarf (1550s onward) and muffler (1590s onward) are the older terms. Comforter is characteristic of the 19th century.

derivation obscure, probably from French *escarpe*, *escharpe*; comforter, descriptive, comforting in cold weather; muffler possibly from Old French *enmofler*.

Stevenage Knitting Co
Ltd, uniform scarf for
Queen Mary's High School
for Girls, Walsall
Knitted wool
British, *c.*1965
V&A: Misc.345–1984

Headscarf
Printed flock nylon
European, 1960–69
V&A: B.151–1999

school uniform garments signifying pupils of a particular educational establishment. For the earliest school uniforms see **_charity uniform_**. At non-charity schools, many of them founded in the 19th century, pupils had no uniforms, but wore their own clothes. However, more and more schools adopted complete uniforms in their own colours, often with a motto and song, to give a sense of school identity. Sports competitions between schools popularized the wearing of identifying colours, 'Now each house has its own uniform of [football] cap and jersey, of some lively colour' (T. Hughes, *Tom Brown's Schooldays*, 1857)

and many of the uniform garments were derived from sportswear, including gymslips, ties, scarves, caps and blazers. Some schools have tried regulating by colour rather than by garment, e.g. in 1977 a school in Lowestoft, Suffolk, adopted a regulation of wearing garments of red, white and/or blue in keeping with that year's Silver Jubilee of Queen Elizabeth II. School uniforms are currently enjoying something of a revival, largely on the grounds that they help with discipline.

dates in the non-charity format, late 19th century to present day.

derivation descriptive.

School uniform dress, blazer and hat, Burlington Grammar School for Girls, London Printed cotton, wool British, 1965–70 V&A: Misc.373–374&A–1984

Scotch suit, Scottish suit

a commercially made boy's version of Highland
dress. Elements included:

kilt a short pleated skirt with wrapover front
(as often in children's clothing, attached to
a bodice for easier wear), the front fastened
with a *kilt pin*.

plaid a length of fabric, usually in a clan
tartan, worn looped about the body and
hanging down from the shoulder.

sgian dubh literally 'dark or black knife', a
dagger worn tucked into the top of one stocking.

sporran a pouch with the front flap decorated
with animal hair or skin, often with silver
mounts, and worn on a strap around the waist
or hips.

Scotch suit
Velvet, wool and cotton
with metal
British, 1870
V&A: Misc.351(1–6)–1979

Other accessories might include a *glengarry
bonnet* or *tam-o'-shanter*, argyle patterned
socks, buckled shoes, a cairngorm brooch and
a spray of heather. *Also called* **Highland suit**
dates 1850s–1920s, thereafter surviving as
pageboy outfits for weddings.
derivation adapted from the clan dress of
the Scottish Highlands.

Scout uniform *see Appendix 2*

scratch mitten *see mitten*

scrunch, **scrunchie**, **scrunchy** an elasticated loop of fabric (structurally a closed tube) for holding the hair together, usually in a bun or ponytail.

dates 1990s onward (scrunching as a hair styling technique is recorded slightly earlier, in 1983).

derivation from the verb *to scrunch* (as implied in compressing the hair into the loop), a word which the OED relates to a number of different verbs, notably *crunch*, *crush* and *cringe*, many of which are from dialect or are onomatopoeic.

semmit *see vest*

Scrunch
Nylon velvet
British, 2007
V&A: MoC

shawl 1 a piece of knitted, crocheted or woven fabric, usually triangular (or square folded into a triangle), wrapped around the upper body for warmth. Up to the 1920s, for the poorer child, a shawl would have to take the place of a coat, while in better-off families, adults often wrapped children in shawls as extras: '... fuzzy, tickly, Shetland shawls were put over our mouths, so that we should not catch cold when we went home through the Cambridge fog' (G. Raverat, *Period Piece*, 1954). **2** a piece of knitted or woven fabric, usually a large square folded into a triangle and wrapped round a baby for warmth. *Also called* **baby shawl**, **blanket**. For the conversion of a baby shawl to a carrying cape, see **carrying cape hug-me-tight** a small triangular baby shawl (Bestway *Knitted Babythings* booklet 1935–50).

dates 1750 onward.

derivation Persian *shāl*.

shearling coat *see furs*

shell suit *see tracksuit*

shift *see chemise*

shimmy *see chemise*

Shawl
Knitted and
crocheted wool
French, 1920–29
V&A: B.149–1999

shirt a front-fastening garment with sleeves, to cover the upper half of the body; regarded as underwear until the introduction of the vest in the middle of the 19th century, and sometimes (particularly by boys), worn so long as to constitute 'shirt-drawers', when the tails were wrapped between the legs instead of wearing separate underpants. Adopted later by girls and women to wear for school and work.

dress shirt (when heavily starched sometimes referred to as a **boiled shirt**) a linen or cotton shirt, usually white, sometimes with a closed and pleated front and a back fastening. '... boys will, without scruple, wear a flannel shirt all day, and a dress white shirt for dinner, with no thought of colds or coughs' (*Myra's Journal*, 1 January 1879).

first shirt a simple front-opening garment for the youngest babies, with vestigial sleeves, and flaps at the centre to fold down over a binder or petticoat, in use from the 18th century, finally going out of use by about 1920.

grandad shirt a 1960s revival of a once-standard form, a shirt with a neckband but without a permanently attached collar.

habit shirt a long-sleeved but very short shirt with tapes around the chest, originally (in the 18th century) for women and girls to wear with a riding habit, and from about 1800 (when it was sometimes known as a chemisette) popular as a fill-in for the low neck of a dress.

dates from about 1000 onward.

derivation from Old English *scyrte*, a short garment.

Wm Sugden & Sons Ltd,
Water Lane brand,
Utility Scheme shirt
Printed cotton
British, 1942–52
V&A: Misc.915–1993

First shirt
Linen
British, 1875–1900
V&A: Misc.252–1982

Bottom
Habit shirt
Linen
British, 1810–15
V&A: T.58A-1972

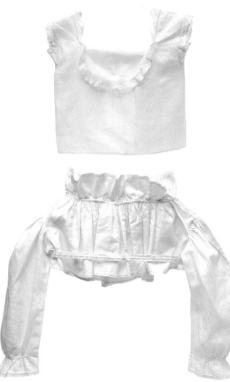

shoe an outer covering for the foot only (as opposed to a boot, which also covers some part of the area above the foot).
dates 10th century onward.
derivation Old English *scōh*, of Germanic origin.

Curiosity Shop
(brand) shoes
Cotton and vinyl
British, 1975–85
V&A: B.366(1,2)–1993

Bottom
Shoes
Morocco leather
with silver
British, 18th century
V&A: T.23(&A,B,C)–1956

short coating, **shortening** the point at which a baby ceased to wear long clothes and was dressed in shorter ones. In the 18th century this took place at about twelve months. Pye Henry Chavasse in 1870 suggests two months. Elizabeth Craig in *Elizabeth Craig's Needlecraft* (1947) comments that many mothers dress their babies in short clothes from birth. Initially, the change was often effected by shortening the skirts of the long clothes, although this could produce a rather clumsy result, especially where a skirt front included *robings*. Some preferred to take the skirt off the bodice and put back the lower part only. *Also called* **tucking up**
dates at least 1790s–1950s.
derivation descriptive (coat in the sense of 'main garment').

Short coating dress
Embroidered lawn
British, 1800–1820
V&A: Misc.54–1985

shorts originally trousers finishing just above or below the knee; later shorts, for sports or leisure wear, sometimes finished at the mid- or upper thigh.

bib shorts shorts with a flap across the chest and straps to fasten at the back, usually for younger children or girls, from the 1920s onward.

cycling shorts close-fitting shorts, latterly made of lycra or similar fabric, a fashion item in the 1990s.

dates first recorded use 1904 (OED).

derivation from 'short trousers'.

Harrods Ltd, suit
with short trousers
Cotton and linen blend
British, 1935–55
V&A: MoC

shroud the garment worn for burial; originally a sheet or length of cloth wound round the entire corpse and sometimes tied around the ankles. Many pre-1800 representations of dead babies, which are assumed to be in shrouds, in fact show the swaddling clothes of the living child, particularly when accompanied by other dead persons in normal dress. While some continued to be buried in their own clothes, by the beginning of the 17th century, representations of dead children increasingly show them in grave clothes, such as caps and gowns (as in, for example the 1674 stoneware 'portrait' of Lydia Dwight in the V&A collections (V&A: 1055–1871). The gowns often show sleeves with wide cuffs folded back, and sometimes hoods, all of which were usually pulled forward before burial to cover the hands and face. From the 1850s onward, the word *shroud* increasingly signified a garment, often resembling a high-necked long-sleeved nightgown. In some families a nightgown was therefore used to save money. A settlement worker in the East End of London in the 1920s was told by a resident that she had no nightgowns left for her new baby because she had had three but used them to bury her three previous children.

dates the association of the word with burial is not recorded until 1570: the custom of wrapping the body for burial was in existence from ancient times, although not universally followed.

derivation Old English *scrúd*, 'textile, garment'.

Figure of Lydia Dwight
in her burial garments
Salt-glazed stoneware
British, 1674
V&A: 1055–1871

shrug, **shrug jacket** a length of knitted fabric, sometimes partly closed, with a cuff at each end, usually worn as a light cardigan or bedjacket. *Also called* **bed scarf**
dates 1930s–1950s.
derivation descriptive of the manner in which it was put on, like a shrug of the shoulders.

singlet *see vest*

Shrug
Knitted wool
British, 1930–39
V&A: Misc.684–1986

siren suit, **air-raid suit** an all-in-one garment, of long-sleeved top and trousers combined, usually made of a warm fabric, sometimes with a hood, 'a cross between pyjamas and a child's rompers' recalled James Leasor in 1955 (Noel Streatfeild, ed., *The Years of Grace*), allegedly invented by wartime Prime Minister Winston Churchill, who wore them himself. The garment was obviously of considerable help in clothing young children, whose siren suits were sometimes knitted from unravelled garments, but ironically it was excluded from commercial manufacture for this age group under Board of Trade regulations in 1944 as being a short-lived fashion garment.
dates D.H. Evans were selling girls' siren suits, in olive green 'proofed suedette', as early as September 1939; the garment continued in use throughout the war, and is arguably the precursor of the snowsuit, as well as the catsuit, jumpsuit and flying suit of the 1960s.
derivation from the alarm siren sounded in Britain during the Second World War to warn civilians to take cover in an air-raid shelter during a bombing raid. As this frequently happened at night, the siren suit was a quick and easy way of getting dressed.

Siren suit
Wool
British, *c*.1940
V&A: Misc.101–1984

sister frocks two or more girls' dresses of different styles in identical fabrics, or of identical style in different fabrics, as worn by siblings. There does not appear to have been an equivalent for brothers. Brother-sister, mother-daughter and father-son garments did exist (e.g. Robin 1209 knitting pattern for father and son lumber jackets) but were never very popular in Britain. Dressing same-gender siblings, even of different ages, in identical garments is very much more common. It is visible in child portraiture from at least the early modern period onward and persists to the present day, and applies to home-made clothes as well as shop-bought ones. 'Mum dressed us up in matching clobber as soon as he [his brother, two years younger] was on two legs.

Strangers would come up to her and ask "Ooh, are they twins?" as if to pander to her insane but not uncommon little fantasy … the same tops, trousers, trainers – even *ties* for Christmas Day' (Andrew Collins [born 1965], *Where Did It All Go Right?*, 2003).

dates the concept is undoubtedly older, but the phrase probably dates from the early years of the 20th century: 'Sister frocks – all smart young moderns are wearing them! They are dresses in the same material … but an individual design for each' (Harvey Nichols catalogue, 1934).

derivation descriptive.

Sister frocks
Printed rayon
British, *c.*1930
V&A: Misc.486(1–2)–1986

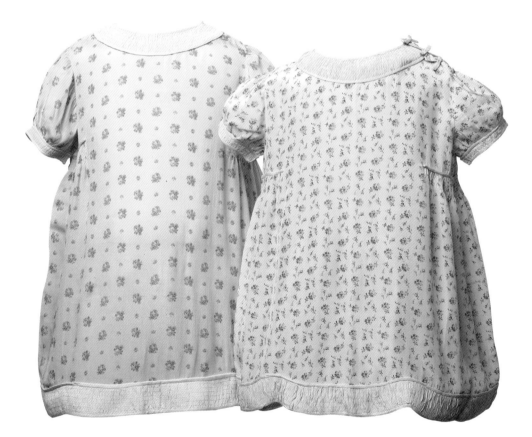

skeleton suit, **skeletons** a close-fitting jacket and trousers buttoning together at the chest or waist. The writer Charles Dickens described them in as 'cloth cases in which small boys used to be confined' (*Sketches by Boz*, 1836). Born in 1812, he was probably speaking from the experience of having worn them himself as a child.

dates 1790s–1830s.

derivation descriptive, both in reference to closeness of fit, and also to the pared-down nature of most versions (skeleton from the Greek *skeletos*, 'dried up').

skirt the lower part of a dress, hanging from the waist, or later a similar garment in its own right. The latter probably evolved from the fashions of the 1880s, with their frequent use of contrasting fabrics, and along with the shirt, became part of the accepted wear of the schoolgirl, the sportswoman and the working girl in the 1890s and 1900s.

underskirt a petticoat, sometimes intended to be visible.

dates as a general term, often in the plural form of skirts, from about 1300 onward; as a separate item for girls, from about 1900.

derivation from Old English *scyrte*, a short garment.

skort a skirt combined with shorts; in girls' clothing originally a novelty garment, but increasingly used for athletic pursuits. Some examples consist of a pair of shorts with a front skirt panel, others are a skirt with an attached pair of shorts beneath.

dates 1980s, revived in the late 1990s.

derivation combination of *skirt* and *shorts*.

slacks *see **trousers***

Skeleton suit
Nankeen
British, early 19th century
V&A: T.165 & A–1915

Opposite
Skirt
Mixed-fabric patchwork
British, 1950–55
Misc.433–1986

sleep suit, **sleeping suit** a one-piece garment, combining pyjama jacket and trousers, usually with some kind of between-the-legs fastening or drop panel at the back. **dates** from at least the 1880s (Allin's advertisement in *Myra's Journal*, 1 April 1884). **derivation** descriptive.

sleeping vest *see nightclothes*

Selfridges advertisement
for a sleeping suit
Printed paper
British, 1932
V&A: MoC

sleeve a covering for all or part of the arm; either a separate entity for attachment to, or a permanently attached part of, a body-garment; detachable sleeves were still in use for babies in the 18th century in conjunction with swaddling, see Foundling Hospital lists 1742 and 1759 in *Appendix 1*.

armlet a separate additional covering for either the forearm or the whole arm, to wear over a sleeve for warmth (*The Workwoman's Guide*, 1838). **dates** 10th century onward. **derivation** Old English *slēfe*, *slēf(e)*, 'sleeve or covering'.

slide comb *see hairslide*

Dress with
detachable sleeves
Wool
British, c.1850
V&A: T.83 & A,B,C–1966

slip 1 a type of dress for a baby or young child. In 1768, the year of her second son's birth, Lady Shelburne had four slips made for him, and another four in the following year. **2** *see* *petticoat*

dates approximately 1700–1830.

derivation from the Middle Low German *slippen*, 'to slip' (with reference to ease of putting on), or possibly in the sense of something narrow.

Slip baby dress
Printed cotton
British, 1810–20
V&A: B.174–1993

slipper a lightweight slip-on shoe, usually with a flat heel or no heel, mainly for indoor use.

bedroom slipper a slipper usually made of fabric.

Norwegian slipper an inexpensive all-felt slipper with imitation fur trim. Children's sizes were advertised at one shilling and sixpence a pair by J. Theobald & Co. in *Myra's Journal*, 1 March 1886.

dates medieval times to present day.

derivation as *slip,* above.

sloppy joe *see sweater*

small clothes, **smallcothes**, **smalls** *see underwear*

Dunlop, slippers
Wool with rubber
British, 1950–59
V&A: Misc.326&A–1979

smock, **smock-frock 1** a traditional garment, worn principally by agricultural workers (including boys), and usually of drab-coloured or greyish cloth, with the fabric gathered in vertical lines across the chest and back. All the parts of the garment were squares, rectangles or triangles, thereby avoiding waste in cutting curved shapes and doing away with the need for a paper pattern. Two 19th-century paintings in the V&A Museum of Childhood collections show boys in smocks: John Morgan's 1865 painting *Snowballing* shows realistically depicted garments; by contrast, the boy in A.D. Fripp's watercolour painting *The Piping Shepherd* has a viridian green smock which owes more to the Aesthetic movement than to anything worn by a real farm worker. **2** *aesthetic clothing* borrowed heavily from this traditional garment, and it was later fashionable for young children of both sexes. **3** an undergarment, *see* *chemise* **dates 1** *c.*1700–1900. **2** *c.*1900 onward. **derivation** Old English *smoc*.

snake belt *see belt*

sneaker *see plimsoll*

Liberty & Co, smock dress
Printed lawn
British, *c.*1930
V&A: B.300–1996

Rural smock
Drabbet
British, 1860–69
V&A: Misc.96–1982

snood originally a form of hairband, but from about 1860 best known as a bag-shaped hairnet with a wide mesh, attached to a hair band or ribbon.

dates from medieval times onward.

derivation Old English *snōd*, of obscure origin.

snorkel, **snorkel coat**, **snorkel jacket**, **snorkel parka** *see parka*

snow heel a shaped piece of knitted fabric put over the heel of a boot or shoe to prevent slipping in icy or snowy conditions.

dates illustrated in *The Workwoman's Guide* (1838), where they are described as being 'particularly good for old people and children', but the practice of putting anti-slip fabric around footwear dates back to at least the Middle Ages.

derivation descriptive.

Snood depicted on a doll
Bisque
German, *c.*1868
V&A: Misc.175–1976

snowsuit, **snow bunny** an all-in-one jacket and trouser combination, or two separate garments, sometimes with closed feet, for young children; usually in fur fabric or waterproof fabric (sometimes quilted). *Also called* **pixie suit**, **comfi suit**, **lumber suit**, all with pixie hoods.
dates 1940s onward.
derivation descriptive.

Snow suit
Fur fabric
British, *c.*1963
V&A: Misc.798(1)–1988

sock a short stocking; often knitted, the earliest versions normally to calf level.
knee sock, **ankle sock** indicate length. Confusingly, knee-length or longer socks have also been referred to as stockings. 'The socks, or stockings, for winter ought to be either lambs'-wool or worsted [a woollen yarn]: it is absurd to wear *cotton* socks or stockings all year round' (Pye Henry Chavasse, *Advice to a Mother*, 1870).
bedsock, **bed sock** one of a pair of socks to keep the feet warm in bed. Originally of knitted wool, modern examples are often made in fleece fabric. 'Bed socks are very necessary for children. They keep them from drawing up their feet into cramped positions' (Chilprufe catalogue, 1922). Presumably the cramped positions were an attempt to warm cold feet.
bunny top a novelty knee-length sock with a fur edging at the knee, briefly fashionable in the 1960s.
hamster sock a vestigial sock, supposed to be invisible, to give a barefooted appearance.
popsock a short version of a nylon stocking, elasticated at the top, popular from the 1960s onward.
toe sock a sock with spaces for individual toes, similar to the finger spaces of a glove.
dates earlier used to refer to various forms of slipper and sandal, but in the modern sense, from medieval times onward.
derivation Old English *socc* from Latin *soccus*.

W.H. Morley, socks
Knitted wool
British, 1851
V&A: T.62&C–1959

sou'wester, **souwester** a waterproof hat, usually of oilskin, and sometimes worn with an oilskin coat (also known as 'oilskins' or 'oilies').

dates at least 1830s onward. Dickens refers to 'slop-sellers' shops, with Guernsey shirts, sou'wester hats, and canvas pantaloons' in *Dombey and Son* (1848).

derivation abbreviation of *south wester*, from south westerly wind which often brings rain.

spat, **spatterdash** *see gaiter*

Waiting for the Skipper,
by Edwin Bale
Painting of a boy
in a sou'wester
British, 1871
V&A: 1167–1886

spencer 1 a short, close-fitting jacket with long sleeves worn by women and children (young children's spencers fastened at the back). **2** a long-sleeved vest-like garment worn between underclothes and outer clothes. In *Testament of Youth* (1933) Vera Brittain (b. 1893) lists her school uniform underclothes: '… and often, in addition, a long-sleeved high-necked knitted woollen "spencer".'

dates 1 1799–1830s and later revived (OED). **2** printed mentions 1881–1972 (OED).

derivation probably named after George John Spencer, 2nd Earl Spencer (1758–1834).

sporran *see Scotch suit*

Spencer
Velvet with lace
British, *c.*1840
V&A: Misc.9(23)–1977

stayband a long piece of fabric used in swaddling to keep a baby's head in position, sometimes double-curved in shape. *Also called* **long stay**

dates 16th century to 18th century.

derivation *stay* probably from Old French *estayer*, 'to prop', plus *band*.

Stayband on a swaddled baby, 1587
From *Children on Brasses*
by John Page Phillips
Printed paper
(London, 1970)

staybodice a bodice for a baby or young child, usually made of corded or quilted fabric and worn as a forerunner of the corset.

dates *c.*1800 onward.

derivation *stay* as in *stayband* above; *bodice* from the phrase 'a pair of bodies' where *body* (a word of debated origin) means a garment for the upper half of the body.

stays *see* **corsets**

Staybodice
Cotton
British, 1925–35
V&A: Misc.564–1986

stocking a tube of fabric, closed at the toe end, to cover the foot and leg; also used to indicate knee-length or longer socks, especially male.

dates as a word, from the 16th century onward, but in use from medieval times under other names such as *stock*.

derivation from the seldom-used verb *to stock*, in the sense of to cover the leg, which derives from Old English *stoc*, 'trunk, pole'.

stocking cap *see cap*

streetglider *see heely*

Stockings for a girl
Knitted cotton
British, *c.*1850
V&A: T.250&A–1968

Aristoc, stretch suit
Nylon towelling
USA, *c.*1974
V&A: Misc.320–1983

stretch suit an all-in-one suit of stretch towelling for a baby, usually with long sleeves and legs and sometimes enclosed feet. Stretch suits had snap fastenings down the centre front, across the crotch and down the legs, which were at first seen as so much simpler and faster in getting a baby changed or dressed that young mothers were advised to put them on babies for sleepwear (as well as daytime clothing); but by about 1985 the advice was to return to the use of nightgowns as simpler and easier than trying to match up all the fastenings.

Babygro™ originally a brand name for a stretch suit, but later used generically. Implies 'grows with the baby', and so often spelt 'baby-grow' that at the height of its popularity it was sometimes humorously referred to as a 'gro(w)bag' (a medium for growing plants).

babystretch™ a Mothercare brand name for the same garment.

dates 1950s onward (first printed mention of Babygro in 1959).

derivation descriptive.

suit 1 a set of matching, toning or accompanying garments; formerly also known as a **costume**, particularly in the 19th and early 20th centuries. *Myra's Journal of Dress and Fashion*, for example, illustrates numerous 'costumes' usually with romantic, foreign or aristocratic-sounding names, such as 'The Ragusa, Prince Milan and Timor Costumes', for a girl, a boy and a woman respectively (1 September 1876).
three-piece suit a suit that includes a waistcoat as well as jacket and trousers.

trouser suit a jacket or coat with trousers instead of a dress or skirt, for a girl or woman. **2** a single garment which covers as much of the body as is deemed necessary (e.g. **sleeping suit**, **swimsuit**).
dates 15th century onward for men and boys, 18th century onward for women and girls.
derivation originating with *a suit of apparel* or *clothes* from Ancient French *siwte*, which later became *suite*, 'set of things that go together' (still familiar in *en suite* rooms, and a *suit* in cards).

Suit for a boy
Silk and cotton blend
British, *c.*1760
V&A: T.113&A–C–1953

Opposite
Suit for a girl
Velvet and silk
British, 1855–60
V&A: T.138&A–1961

sunbonnet a bonnet with a projecting brim and a neck curtain to give the wearer protection from the sun, originally made of fabric but with later versions in other materials such as straw. 'Make her a Sunbonnet ...', urges 'Mabs' in the August 1931 number of the dressmaking periodical *Children's Dress*; '... with a simple cotton frock a little old-world bonnet ... looks delightful'. From the child's standpoint, however, Sylvia Townsend Warner (born 1894) commented that 'nothing could have reconciled me to being at once blinded, deafened, and half cooked' and always contrived to lose hers until no more were ordered (*Scenes of Childhood and Other Stories*, 1981).
dates traditionally worn by girls and women in the countryside, probably until 1900s, then particularly popular in general use for girls from 1910s to 1950s; still in use for young children in modified form.
derivation descriptive.

Sunday best for many pre-20th-century families, the only opportunity for wearing their best clothes was on Sundays, when manual work was discouraged, and church attendance expected. Eleven-year-old Emily's mother '... bought a length of black serge to make her a Sunday coat' when she took her first job as a nursery maid in the 1880s (a hat was supplied by her employer; Noel Streatfeild, *Gran-Nannie*, 1975).
dates at least 1840s onward.
derivation worn for Sunday churchgoing.

sunglasses eyeglasses with tinted or polarized lenses, whether plain or optically prescribed, to protect the eyes in bright sunlight; originally referred to as **dark glasses**. *Also called* **sunnies**, **sun specs**, **shades**
dates 1920s onward.
derivation descriptive.

Sunbonnet
Printed organza
British, 1925–30
V&A: Misc.75(17)–1976

Sunglasses
Moulded plastic
Hong Kong, 1930–50
V&A: Misc.599–1985

sun hat a hat to give protection against the sun, originally worn in hot climates, and made of pale materials to reduce heat absorption
dates 1870s onward.
derivation descriptive.

sunshade *see parasol*

Sunhat
Sisal fibre
British, 1925–30
V&A: B.653–1993

sunsuit, **sundress** a garment giving the wearer maximum exposure to the sun, unlike *sunglasses*, *sun hat*, *sunshade*, etc., although the two types of 'sun' garment were often worn together.
dates in children's clothing, from about 1920 onward, probably worn earlier and in greater numbers than by adults, at least initially.
derivation descriptive.

superstitions *see traditional and superstitious items*

surf suit *see wet suit*

surf shoe *see beach shoe*

Sunsuit
Cotton
British, 1920–29
V&A: Misc.162(1)–1984

surplice a loose-fitting white linen garment usually worn over a **cassock** by choir members for church services.

dates 13th century onward.

derivation apparently derived similarly to *pelisse*, in reference to the wearing of fur garments in church, and prefixed by *sur* – from French *sur*, 'over, above' – to indicate that it was worn over other garments.

surtout *see coat*

suspender 1 a clip, usually attached to a band or garment, for holding up a stocking or sock. **2** another word for **brace**.

suspender belt an undergarment worn around the waist or hips, incorporating suspenders to hold stockings up, used from 1900s onward. *Also called* **garter belt**

dates 1870s onward.

derivation from Latin *suspendere*, 'to hang'.

Advertisement for
Hoven's suspenders
Printed paper
British, 1879
V&A: MoC

SWAN AND EDGAR, Piccadilly and Regent St., W.

GARTERS ENTIRELY SUPERSEDED.

BY

HOVEN'S IMPROVED PATENT STOCKING SUSPENDER.

It has the following Advantages :—

1. It allows free circulation of the blood.
2. It leaves no mark on the limbs, as made by garters.
3. It holds the stocking up tightly, and *without a wrinkle.*
4. *It cannot tear the stocking* under any circumstances.
5. It *gives* to any movement of the body.
6. It does not *increase* the size around the waist.

PRICES :—**2/6**, 2/9 (Cotton), 4/- (Silk), YOUNG LADIES', 2/2 (Cotton), & 3/6 (Silk), CHILDREN'S 1/6 and 2/6 (Silk).

All Post Orders must be Prepaid, and will be Sent Post Free by Return, Securely Packed in Ornamental Box, by

L. HOVEN & CO., 33, Castle Street, Holborn, London, E.C.

Size of Waist required.

SOCK SUSPENDERS FOR GENTLEMEN very suitable for presents, 1/3 Cotton & 2/- Silk.

swaddling, **swathing, swaddling** or **swathing bands**, **clothes** or **clouts** strips of linen for wrapping babies, worn with accompanying garments such as first shirt, forehead cloth, caps, mittens, collar, stayband, and long bib. Swaddling was intended to keep the child warm and safely in its resting place, and to help the limbs grow straight.

modern swaddling a one-piece wrap, based on recent academic research, intended to help babies to sleep better and said to have helped to lower instances of Sudden Infant Death Syndrome; other experts argue that swaddling is a form of child abuse and can deprive a child of necessary neurological development.

swathe, **swather**, **sweather** originally another name for a swaddling band, subsequently a *binder*.

dates from ancient times; in Britain and USA only in use until the 18th century, but remaining in use in some countries, e.g. Italy, until the 1930s.

derivation Old English *swathian*, 'to wrap, bandage'.

sweat *see sweatshirt*

Swaddling band
Embroidered linen
French, 18th century
V&A: B.13–2001

sweater a knitted tunic-like garment, usually with long sleeves; now more or less synonymous with *jersey*, *jumper*, *pullover*.

sloppy joe a very loose-fitting sweater, originally from the USA, early 1940s to about 1963.

dates at least 1850s onward.

derivation from *sweat*. Sweaters were originally worn to cause extra weight loss while exercising, later to prevent catching cold before or after exercise, and subsequently came into general use.

Sweater
Knitted wool
Norwegian, 1960–69
V&A: Misc.225–1986

sweatshirt, **sweat** (the latter mainly US) originally a close-fitting long-sleeved sweater-like garment with a reinforced neck panel, made from fleece-backed cotton. Pasolds made the earliest British children's version as part of their Ladybird range, although calling the garment a 'sweater' like their knitted yarn garments (autumn 1960 price list).
dates 1930s onward in USA, 1950s onward in Britain.
derivation a *sweater* made like a *shirt* (in fabric, not knitted).

Swimsuit
Printed cotton
European, 1955–65
V&A: Misc.566-1986

swimming costume, **swimming trunks**, **swimsuit** a garment or garments for wear in the sea or other body of water. The bathing suit was the earlier form, reflecting the fact that bathing was generally a dip in the water for health or hygienic reasons, rather than the exercise of a swim, thus the early versions were substantial in order to preserve not only the modesty but also the body temperature of people who were accustomed to wear layers of clothing at all times. Boys would sometimes strip naked to bathe. In 1800 Samuel Taylor Coleridge wrote about his three-year-old son Hartley to a friend that 'This afternoon I sent him naked into a shallow of the river Greta; he trembled with the novelty, yet you cannot conceive his raptures'. The custom was already centuries old, as shown in the August calendar page of the *Très Riches Heures* of the Duc de Berry (*c*.1415; Musée Condé, Chantilly), and in Brueghel's painting *Children's Games* (1560; Kunsthistorischesmuseum, Vienna), and continued for some time even after the introduction of bathing costumes, but was always considered unacceptable for girls.
Also called **bathing costume**, **bathing dress**, **bathing suit**
dates the modern idea of the bathing costume dates from about the 1870s.
derivation descriptive.

swing coat see **coat**

Swiss belt, **Swiss waistband** see **belt**

Bathing suit
Printed cotton
British, 1870–79
V&A: Misc.102-1986

tabard in childrenswear, a type of double-sided apron, fastening at the side, originally an outdoor garment, now most commonly worn for art activities or dressing up for younger children.

dates the apron meaning of the word appears to be early 20th century.

derivation from Old French *tabart*.

tailclout *see nappy*

tam-o'-shanter, **tamoshanter**, **tam**, **tammy**, **tammie**, **tam-o'-shanter bonnet** or **cap** a large circular woollen hat with a flat crown, of traditional Scottish origin.

dates as a fashion, particularly for children, 1880s onward.

derivation from the name of the main character in Robert Burns's 1790 poem *Tam O'Shanter*, who is shown in the earliest illustrations wearing one on his head.

Tabard apron
Printed cotton
British, *c.*1927
V&A: Misc.954–1993

Tam-o'-shanter, uniform hat,
St Mary's High School
for Girls, Walsall
Knitted wool
British, *c.*1965
V&A: Misc.346–1984

tank, **tank top** 1 originally a short, close-fitting knitted jumper, sleeveless or with short sleeves, usually for wear over a shirt or blouse. **2** a strappy top.

dates 1 1965 onward, but at its most fashionable 1968–75. **2** 1970s onward, particularly characteristic of the USA.

derivation origin unclear, but possibly based on *tank suit*, a swimming costume with a scoop neck, where tank is a reference to a body of water such as a pool.

tankini *see* **bikini**

teddy *see* **camiknickers**

teenform *see* **bra**

thong, **g-string**, **v-string** a minimal covering for the genital area, held in place with cord or braid ties or loops. In Western childrenswear, usually worn by girls, and sometimes sold as part of a set with a training bra.

dates thongs are traditional wear in many cultures; their adoption as a fashion item in the West dates from the 1970s.

derivation Old English *thwang*, *thwong*.

three-piece suit *see* **suit**

Lister/Lee Target knitting pattern for tank tops
Printed paper
British, *c*.1975
V&A: Misc.91(16)–1985

tie a narrow band of fabric worn around the neck, usually in conjunction with a *collar*, to the extent that 'collar and tie' is often cited as an acceptable standard of smart male dress; collars and ties have also been an important part of *school uniform* for both boys and girls. 'The … brown-and-white checked ginghams, which were the summer uniform of the school … looked very fresh and crisp … the girls wore the flame-coloured school ties with them' – Elinor M. Brent-Dyer's description of the uniform of her fictional Chalet School, but also of the school which she herself ran from 1938–48, the Margaret Roper School in Hereford. *Also called* **necktie**, **neck-tie**

Marks & Spencer, tie
Knitted terylene
British, 1966–8
V&A: Misc.1006–1992

bow tie a tie in the form of a bow, often worn by young boys, especially in made-up form as being easier than knotting a long tie. Boys in the 19th century sometimes wore a length of ribbon as a substitute. Dorry, aged about ten in *What Katy Did at School* (set in 1868) comes to his eldest sister and asks her to 'fasten the blue ribbon under his collar … he was very particular as to the size of the bows and length of the ends, and made her tie and retie more than once'.

kipper tie one of exaggeratedly wide cut (1965–75).

dates 1830s onward.

derivation descriptive of the action of fastening it around the neck.

Bertie and Harold
Stone in bow ties,
by W.H. Palmer
Photographic print
British, *c*.1895
V&A: MoC

tights an all-in-one combination of a pair of stockings with a knicker-like garment, usually all of the same fabric, but sometimes with the 'knickers' of cotton. Tights are normally closed at the foot end, but the wearing of footless tights has sometimes been borrowed from dancers' practice clothing from the 1970s onward. *Also called* (US) **pantyhose**

dates tights had been worn in a theatrical context since at least the 1830s, but in the modern sense of everyday underwear are characteristic of the early 1960s to the present day.

derivation from the close fit (the earliest *tights* were men's close-fitting breeches).

tippet a short cape, often with long pointed tips at the front, for women and girls; also an important element of girls' charity school uniform, where it was sometimes worn fastening at the back.

dates medieval in origin, still popular during the 19th century.

derivation of uncertain origin, but possibly from the tips.

toe sock *see sock*

Gel brand, tights for a girl
Nylon
French, 1960–69
V&A: B.143–1999

Tippet
Printed cotton
British, *c*.1840
V&A: Misc.9(22B)–1977

toe the line the slogan of a range of Norvic brand children's shoes designed to be used in conjunction with an X-ray machine called a pedascope. Each shoe contained a strip of metal calculated to show where a child's toes should come to in order to allow a good fit but with optimum room for growth. When the child put the shoes on and stood inside the pedascope, it showed whether the toes were over the metal strip, in which case the shoes were too small.
dates introduced in about 1949; discontinued in about 1969 when there was a scare about X-rays damaging children's feet.
derivation descriptive.

top hat *see hat*

Norvic, 'toe the line' shoes
Leather
British, *c.*1949
V&A: Misc.258&A–1979

topknot a fashionable decoration for the hair or cap, consisting of a small bunch of ribbons, flowers, jewels, lace, etc. *Also called* **pompon**, **pompom**, **pompadour**
dates mainly 1700s–1760s.
derivation Old English *top(p)* and similar words in many other North European languages, which include references to plumes of feathers as well as the crown of the head; *knot* in the sense of a knot of ribbons, from Old English *cnotta. Pompon* and *pompom* are French for various types of ornament for wear; *pompadour* is from the name of the Marquise de Pompadour (1721–64), mistress of Louis XV of France, who inspired a number of fashions.

toreador pants *see trousers*

tow coat *see duffel coat*

Painting of a girl
wearing a topknot,
by an unknown artist
Oil on canvas
British, *c.*1730
V&A: Misc.199–1990

tracksuit a soft fabric jacket and trousers, originally worn by athletes before and after sporting activity. For young children it was occasionally an all-in-one garment, e.g. Mothercare autumn/winter catalogue 1969–70; the Ladybird catalogue for spring 1962 shows one described as a 'tracker'.

shell suit a tracksuit with a shell of shiny synthetic waterproof fabric over a soft lining, popular in the 1980s and '90s.

dates 1960s onward as a fashion item.

derivation descriptive, from athletics track.

Clothkits, tracksuit
Towelling
British, 1981
V&A: Misc.312(1,2)–1981

traditional and superstitious

items among the traditions and superstitions concerning the benefits of various fabrics and colours are: the use of sheepskin to line shoes; coral, animal claws and bone as amuletic jewellery to assist teething; the colour red as representative of blood and the life force, to give strength and aid recovery from illness; and the colour blue as protection, from its association first with the sky spirits and later with the Virgin Mary.

trainer pants, training pants

waterproof or thick fabric knickers with an absorbent inner layer for babies to wear during potty or toilet training. 'As no bulky nappies are used, baby can look smart when dressed without any fear of embarrassment to parents … With pneumatic banding at legs and waist, soiling during the training period is contained within the pants' (Mothercare autumn/winter catalogue 1969–70).

dates 1960s onward.

derivation descriptive.

Wm Baker (Leicester) Ltd,
Beautex brand,
trainer pants
Towelling
British, c.1963
V&A: Misc.836(2)–1988

trainer, **training shoe** a non-spiked lace-up athletics shoe, later a fashion item, originally of leather, said to be the invention of Adi Dassler, founder of the Adidas brand. Later variations include synthetic materials, different styles of shoe, separate compartments for the big toe, and different fastenings, including straps.

flashlight trainer a trainer with built-in lights activated by the wearer's footsteps. *See also* **heely**

dates 1960s onward.

derivation originally for wear during sports *training*.

training bra see **bra**

trappa kap see **cap**

trews see **trousers**

tricorne, **tricorne hat** a later name for the three-cornered hat fashionable during the 18th century.

dates mainly 1700–1790.

derivation French, literally three-horned or pronged; like **bicorne**, the term was not contemporary with the hats.

trouser suit see **suit**

Converse All Stars™ trainers
Canvas and rubber
British, 2007
V&A: MoC

Tricorne hat for 'Lord Clapham' doll
Felt
British, 1695–1700
V&A:T.847(M)–1974

Bottom
LA Gear Inc., flashlight training shoes
Vinyl and nylon
USA/Indonesia, 1992
V&A: Misc.213(1,2)–1996

trousers a bifurcated garment covering the lower torso and each leg down to the ankle. *Also called* **slacks**, (US) **pants**
Euphemisms **ineffibles**, **inexpressibles**, **nether integuments** and **unmentionables** were sometimes considered more polite usage than trousers or drawers, mainly in the 19th and early 20th centuries.

boot-cut trousers trousers with a medium-flared lower leg, so called from being wide enough to accommodate the wearing of fashion boots beneath them, popular from the 1990s onward.

capris, **capri pants** cropped close-fitting trousers with a vent at the hem, mainly fashionable in the 1950s and early 1960s; named after the Mediterranean island of Capri, a fashionable holiday destination. The writer Bill Bryson (born 1951) recalls his disorganized mother persuading him to wear his sister's capri pants: 'They were a brilliant lime green, very tight, and had little slits at the bottom … "This can't be right, Mom," I said. "These are Betty's old Capri pants, aren't they?" "No, honey," my mom replied soothingly. "They're *pirate* pants. They're very fashionable"' (*The Life and Times of the Thunderbolt Kid*, 2007).

cargo pants, **cargo trousers** trousers with numerous additional pockets (potentially for carrying 'cargo') in the legs; probably of US military origin, and fashion items from the 1980s onward.

chinos trousers (originally made in the 1930s) of chino fabric, a kind of twilled cotton of a light brown or khaki colour (from Latin American Spanish *chino*, 'toasted', referring to the colour).

combat or **kombat trousers** or **pants** military-style trousers originally available as army surplus in the 1950s, then as fashion garments marketed in camouflage pattern (and at times known as camouflage trousers) but now available in many colours.

oval trousers long (often floor-length) baggy trousers with an exaggeratedly low crotch, popular from the late 1980s onward; possibly named from the deep oval shape of the body.

palazzo pants wide-legged, full length trousers for women and girls, often exaggeratedly wide legged for dancing, fashionable from the mid-1990s. The connection with the Italian word *palazzo*, 'palace', is unclear.

toreador pants close-fitting trousers, just below knee-length, resembling Capri pants, and fashionable at much the same time (inspired by the breeches worn by the *toreador*, or bull-baiter, in Spanish bullfights).

trews trousers based on the traditional Gaelic forms of trouser; in modern commercial usage often signifying trousers of plaid or tartan fabric.

ufo trousers trousers with many attached straps of self fabric, fashionable from the 1990s onward; possibly so called because considered to be a fantasy look, or because of the flying strips of fabric.

dates 1770s onward.

derivation extension (perhaps to suggest a pair) of *trouse*, from Gaelic *triubhas*.

Trousers
Wool
British, 1856
V&A: T.70(B)–1929

trowsers 1 old-fashioned spelling of *trousers*. **2** another word for *pantalettes*. 'Mrs Kenwigs, too, was quite a lady in her manners, and of a very genteel family … the two eldest of her little girls … had flaxen hair, tied with blue ribbons, hanging in luxuriant pigtails down their backs; and wore little white trousers with frills round the ankles' (Dickens *The Life and Adventures of Nicholas Nickleby*, 1839).

trunks, **trunk drawers** boys' close-fitting underpants with short extended legs and button-through placket fastening at the front. **swimming trunks** *see swimming costume*
dates originally the bifurcated garment worn with a doublet; in the modern sense 1920s–50s.
derivation unclear, possibly *trunk* in either its sense of the lower part of the body, or a pipe or hollow covering.

British Home Stores Ltd,
swimming trunks
Nylon
British, 1970–79
V&A: Misc.439–1981

T-shirt, **tee shirt** a top originally
resembling an early 20th-century vest or
undershirt, characteristically with a round
neck, short sleeves and no fastenings.
T-shirt dress a dress made from the
same fabric as a T-shirt, and cut along
the same lines.
dates certainly in existence from the 1920s,
but not widely used until the 1940s (USA) and
1950s (Ladybird was one of the first ranges of
children's clothes in Britain to include T-shirts).
derivation from the T-shaped outline of the
garment when flat, although in modern usage
the word has extended to almost any top made
of machine-knitted cotton, whether T-shaped
or not.

tucking up *see short coating*

Marks & Spencer,
T-shirt dress
Knitted cotton fabric
British, 1980
V&A: Misc.434–1985

tucker a lace or cloth frill, usually white,
worn 'tucked' inside the neck of a dress,
especially where the neckline is low; once so
typical that the phrase 'best bib and tucker'
(where 'bib' refers to either a similar article
or the bib of an apron) was in widespread use
by the 18th century for 'best clothes'. Tuckers
used in children's dress were often limited to a
single frill of lace attached to a narrow tape or
ribbon. A contemporary portrait of the original
child owner of dress T.403–1971 in the V&A
Museum of Childhood's collection shows that
the simple tucker surviving on the dress (see
illustration below) is likely to be the same one.
dates 17th to 19th century, '… her only comfort
was the knowledge that the modest tucker
drawn up round the plump shoulders was
real lace' (L.M. Alcott, *An Old Fashioned
Girl*, 1870).
derivation probably linked to middle German and
Dutch *tucken*, *tocken*, 'to move, tuck'.

Sears brand, T-shirt
Polyester-cotton blend
USA, 1978
V&A: Misc.508–1984

Tucker
Lace and cotton
British, *c*.1855
V&A: T.403–1971

tunic a term used to describe a variety of garments, but in children's clothing from 1700 onward, best known as **1** a boy's or man's coat-like garment with long sleeves, a short full skirt and a button-through fastening at the front, often with additional vertical lines of buttons as trimming on the bodice; usually worn over a shirt and wide-legged trousers. **2** short for *gym tunic*, particularly when used for non-sports wear. *See* **gymslip**

dates originally a loose straight garment of varying length worn by both sexes from classical Greek and Roman times. Boys' tunics in the sense of **1** date from the 1840s.

derivation Latin *tunica*.

tuxedo, **tuxedo coat**, **tuxedo jacket** *see* **evening dress**

Tunic
Cotton
British, 1830–40
V&A: T.337–1910

twin set, **twin-set**, **twinset** a matching cardigan and (usually short-sleeved) jumper. Although girls' twin-sets were not expensive – they were a staple of Selfridges bargain basement, and also easily made at home – they were always considered smart. One entry in Selfridges August 1949 catalogue comments: 'A style to educate the Junior fashion sense'.

dates characteristically 1930s–60s.

derivation *twin* to indicate paired garments.

Selfridges illustration
of a twin set
Printed paper
British, 1949
V&A: MoC

uU

ufo trousers *see trousers*

ug boots, **ugg boots**, **Uggs™** a type of flat-heeled soft sheepskin boot resembling a sock, usually with a seam around the front of the ankle.

dates claimed to be in production in Australia since the 19th century; in the UK, early 21st century onward.

derivation originally a brand name but subsequently much imitated, said to be short for 'ugly' and also from 'hug'; the OED Online suggests that it is probably from a series of cartoon characters.

ulster, **ulster overcoat** a long coat of heavy cloth, often with a belt or half-belt at the waist. 'When winter came he bought three of the poorest girls warm, grey ulsters, such as were then fashionable, to go to church in' (F. Thompson, *Lark Rise to Candleford,* set in the 1880s).

ulsterette a lighterweight version of the ulster.

dates 1870s (the OED cites its introduction as the Ulster Overcoat by J.G. McGee & Co. of Belfast, 1867), still available in the late 1930s.

derivation from *Ulster*, Northern Ireland, where it originated.

Uggs™
Suede
Australian, 2007
V&A: MoC

umbrella a frame covered with fabric and attached to a handle; originally a synonym for parasol (sunshade), but subsequently for use in rain only. Even for those who could afford them, many families could only justify one umbrella for general use: child-sized umbrellas were not considered necessary. In an attempt to persuade parents to buy them and children to use them, manufacturers tried using novelty in the making of children's umbrellas. The Army & Navy Stores catalogue (1939–40) lists 'Children's umbrellas. Plain handles. Or with animal heads' priced between six shillings and ninepence and ten shillings and sixpence'.

dates 17th century onward.

derivation from Latin *umbra*, 'shade'.

underpants an undergarment, usually for boys or men, covering the lower part of the torso, a fairly generic term used to describe a variety of forms such as boxer shorts, briefs, trunks, etc.

dates although 'undershirt' and 'undervest' were in use by the mid-19th century, 'underpants' as a word seems not to have appeared until the early 1930s.

derivation descriptive, in the sense of pants to wear under other clothes, rather than something to wear under pants.

©BBC, Tweenies umbrella
Nylon, metal and plastic
British/Chinese, *c.*2000
V&A: MoC

undershirt a long-sleeved woollen vest, with a button-through fastening at the neck.
dates originally a less specific garment (though with the same function), the long-sleeved woollen undershirt described above was principally a 19th-century item.
derivation descriptive. It was specified as *under*shirt because a shirt was originally underwear.

underwear also referred to as **linen**, **smalls** (from *smallclothes* which were breeches and therefore not underwear at all), **déshabille** (colloquial *dissable*, *dizzerbell*) from the French word for undressed, *déshabillé*. Underwear performs the double function of keeping outer clothes cleaner and preventing them from chafing the skin. See **Appendix 4**.
dates a term in use from the late 19th century onward.
derivation descriptive.

Undershirt
Knitted wool fabric
British, c.1850
V&A: Misc.4–1961 (part)

uniform see **charity uniform**, **livery**, **school**, **youth movements**

union suit see **combinations**

unmentionables a mainly 19th-century euphemism for **trousers** or **drawers**.

utility bodice see **liberty bodice**

Utility clothing, **Utility wear**
The Utility Scheme was set up by the British Government during the Second World War as a means of producing various goods, including clothes, economically and without waste, and ensuring (as far as was possible) their fair distribution. *See also* **L-85**
dates 1942–52.
derivation descriptive, to emphasize the message of contribution to the war effort by avoiding waste.

Utility Scheme
coat and hat
Wool
British, 1942–52
V&A: Misc.18&A–1985

vV wW yY zZ

v-string *see thong*

Vandyke suit, Vandyke dress an

imitation or revival of 17th-century styles,
usually in fabrics of luxurious appearance.
The *Fauntleroy suit* was probably its most
successful and longest-lasting version.
dates late 18th century onward. Gainsborough's
1770 portrait of Jonathan Buttall, known
as 'The Blue Boy' (Huntington Art Gallery,
San Marino, California), is one of the most
familiar examples.
derivation from Sir Anthony van Dyck's
numerous portraits of sitters in the original
versions of the styles.

Vandyke dress,
bridesmaid's dress
Satin, ribbon and lace
British, 1903
V&A: Misc.485(1)–1986

veil a translucent covering for the face, usually
made of a sheer fabric such as net. Veils have
had two main uses in children's clothing.
1 for babies. It was formerly thought advisable
to cover a baby's face when taking it outside,
to protect its eyes, and its face in general.
Although veils seem never to be mentioned
in layette lists, they were once in widespread
use for this purpose, even in families of fairly
modest means. When veils became obsolete,
some older carers still felt that a baby's face
should be protected outdoors, and would insist
on substituting a handkerchief or a corner of
the child's shawl. **2** as part of, or an adjunct
to a girl's hat. Louisa M. Alcott adds a veil to
the fashionable outfit fourteen-year-old Rose
Campbell tries on in her novel *Eight Cousins*
(1875): 'A high velvet hat, audaciously turned
up in front, with a bunch of pink roses and
a sweeping plume, was cocked over one ear …
and a spotted veil, tied so closely over her face
that her eyelashes were rumpled by it, gave
the last touch of absurdity to her appearance.'
Girls would not normally wear a veil as
part of evening dress, as women sometimes
did in the early 19th century.
dates 1 probably about 1800–1920.
2 apparently 19th century
only for girls.
derivation various old
French forms such as
veil, veille, related to
Latin *vela* and *velum*,
'sail, curtain or veil'.

Veil for a baby
Embroidered net
British, 1924
V&A: Misc.400–1982

veldtschoen sandals *see sandals*

vest an undergarment, originally with sleeves, to cover the torso, for wear next to the skin. *Also called* **undervest**; *see also* **undershirt**

cellular vest one made of a fabric with a pattern of small holes; cellular fabrics have been available since at least the 1880s, but the cellular vest was probably at its most popular for children from the 1930s to the 1950s.

semmit, semmite, semat, semmet, a mainly Scottish word for a vest. Wilena Hitching gives instructions for a 'vest or semmit' in *Baby-Clothing on Healthful, Economical & Original Lines* (1914).

singlet a low-necked sleeveless vest, originally associated with athletics.

string vest a vest made of a wide mesh fabric resembling string netting, and usually in the form of a singlet, particularly popular in the 1960s and '70s.

dates in this sense, 1850s onward; the function of the vest was formerly supplied by the chemise for girls and the shirt for boys.

derivation from French *veste,* ultimately from Latin *vestis,* 'garment'.

waders in children's clothing, waders were originally waterproof rompers for wear on the beach. In current usage, they consist of waterproof trousers worn to the armpits, with shoulder straps (more like the adult garment), and with waterproof boots attached for the feet.

dates originally over-the-knee waterproof boots, available from the 1840s; the romper version was characteristic of the 1920s and '30s (Selfridges Bargain Basement offered plain and printed versions 'with nursery designs' to fit age one to six years in the late 1920s, at a cost of one shilling and sixpence each).

derivation descriptive.

Vedonis brand, vest
(singlet)
Mercerized cotton
British, c.1940
V&A: Misc.131–1984

Waders
Mackintosh fabric
British, 1928
V&A: Misc.199–1976

waist a dress bodice, originally from the period when dresses were made as a separate bodice and skirt. 'Don't see how two draggled skirts and a stained waist can be transformed into a whole rig' (L.M. Alcott, *An Old-Fashioned Girl*, 1870).
dates 1600s–1900s. In modern usage, surviving in **shirt waist** or **shirt waister dress** a dress with a bodice cut like the upper part of a shirt, particularly fashionable in the 1950s.
derivation according to the OED 'The part of a garment between the shoulders and the "waist" or narrowed part'.

waistbelt *see belt*

Waist
Shot silk
British, *c.*1885
V&A: Misc.58(1)–1985

waistcoat 1 a light underjacket, originally with sleeves, but from the mid-18th century onward, usually sleeveless and becoming shorter until reaching just below the waistline. Both single- and double-breasted styles have been popular. Pye Henry Chavasse, who disapproved of waistcoats in general because they exposed the upper chest, conceded: 'Double-breasted waistcoats cannot be too strongly recommended for *delicate* youths' (*Advice to a Mother*, 1870). *Also called* **weskit** (dialect), **vest** (US). *See also* **cheat**
2 in swaddling, a single wide band about the waist; in an older baby, a type of petticoat.
dates late 17th century onward.
derivation *waist see* **dress bodice**; *coat* in the sense of a garment clothing the sides.

Opposite
Waistcoat
Embroidered satin
British, 1820–9
V&A: Misc.227(4)–1979

walking stick a stick carried while walking, especially as part of a more formal outfit; the commercially made and more highly finished examples were usually carried by boys from better-off families.

dates died out for use by boys during the Second World War. "It will absolutely ruin my walking stick", grumbled Robin [aged fifteen], who was beginning to take an interest in his personal appearance and to be rather particular about his possessions' (M. Pardoe, *Bunkle Began It*, 1942).

derivation descriptive.

Selfridges advertisement
for washing frocks
Printed paper
British, 1948
V&A: MoC

washing frock a dress made of washable fabric (i.e. one that will wash without damaging its colour or finish). Even in the 1930s, fabric manufacturers were still stressing that the washability of their products made them particularly suitable for children's clothes. 'While it is hardly wise to hold kiddies firmly in check, they can play havoc with their clothes. But make their clothes from durable, cheerful "LUVISCA" – a COURTAULD fabric – and boisterous play will have no ill results. Besides strength, this famous fabric offers a complete variety of colours and striped designs, all laundry-safe ...' (advertisement in *Weldon's Bazaar of Children's Fashions*, July 1933).

dates 18th to 20th century.

derivation descriptive.

waterproof pants, plastic pants
see **pilch**

wedding clothes see **bridesmaid('s) dress**, **pageboy suit**

wellington boot, wellington, wellie, welly best known in childrenswear as a cuffless waterproof boot, originally to mid-calf length, but this has always depended to some extent on the size of the child. *Also called* **gum boot**, Jilly Cooper in *Class* suggests that gum boot is a more upper- and upper-middle class usage than any version of the word wellington. **jelly wellies** wellingtons made from plastic (as used for *jelly shoes*).
welly pet a child's waterproof boot with the toe moulded to resemble an animal head, notably a frog.

dates the waterproof version of wellington boot appears to have been introduced from the USA in the 1900s; the term *gum boot* was certainly in use by the 1930s (Eve Garnett, *Holiday at the Dew Drop Inn,* 1971); the original wellington was an adult fashion, a cuffless leather boot worn from 1817 to the 1900s.
derivation *wellington* from Arthur Wellesley, 1st Duke of Wellington (1769–1852); *gum* is short for *gum elastic*, an alternative phrase for rubber, from French *gomme elastique*.

weskit *see* *waistcoat*

Mothercare brand,
wellington boots
pvc
British, 1975–80
V&A: Misc.138(1,2)–1982

Dunlop, 'jelly wellies'
Vinyl
British, 1982
V&A: Misc.228(1,2)–1983

wet suit a close-fitting all-in-one waterproof suit to protect the wearer from cold in the water while surfing, diving, etc. Originally made of rubber, now made of synthetic fibres such as neoprene. The adult garment usually reaches to wrist and ankle, but children's versions, although available in full length, more often have short sleeves and legs reaching to mid-thigh. Their success has also led to the availability of baby-sized and two-piece versions. The suits' growth in popularity as children's beachwear is partly an indication of practicality, since a child can continue to wear one for hours, in and out of the water, without the need to change, and may also indicate a return to protecting children's skin from prolonged exposure to the sun.
Also called **surf suit**
dates 1950s to the present.
derivation descriptive.

whittle a term used for a number of different white garments, mostly wraps such as shawls, mantles, blankets, swathes: '… the first apparayle of children, as, swathes, whittels, wastecoats, and such like …' (Thomas Cooper, *Thesaurus linguæ Romanæ et Brittanicæ*, 1565). Its specific attribution as a large white shawl used to wrap a baby (from a list of baby clothes in Cunnington family correspondence of 1843) is quoted by Phyllis Cunnington and Catherine Lucas in *Costume for Births, Deaths and Marriages* (1972).
dates 16th to 19th century.
derivation Old English *hwítel*, from *hwít*, 'white'.

windcheater *see jacket*

winklepicker, **winkle-picker** a close-fitting shoe with an exaggeratedly long pointed toe. *Also called* **pike**
dates 1950s and early 1960s, revived in the late 1970s and 1990s, although the concept was an old one – excessively long-toed shoes were among the abiding fashions of the medieval period.
derivation humorous reference to the length of the toe being suitable to extract the meat from a winkle.

Wolf Cub, **Cub Scout uniform**
see Appendix 2

Woodcraft Folk *see Appendix 2*

woollie, **wooly** a garment (often a jumper or cardigan) of wool, and usually knitted. 'Baby's woollies will fit well … wash perfectly, and always be as smooth as velvet, in Bairns-Wear wools specially spun for the little ones' (advertisement in *Good Needlework and Knitting* magazine, November 1936). Sometimes used generically for any warm garment or set of garments, as in the phrase 'winter woollies'.
dates 1860s onward.
derivation Old English *wull*.

working clothes the clothing worn by children for work could demand a significant change in their wardrobe, sometimes at considerable expense to their family even when specific garments were not stipulated. While uniforms such as *livery* might be supplied as part of the terms of employment, even the most junior army and navy officers were originally expected to have their own uniforms made. A girl going into employment in a household would generally be expected to bring specified clothes with her or have the cost of supplying them deducted from her wages. The Streatfeild family's nanny began her first job as a nursery-maid, aged eleven, in the 1880s. Her mother bought 'enough print for the two dresses she had to have and a bolt of cotton for her aprons, underwear and caps' (Noel Streatfeild, *Gran-Nannie*, 1975). Work clothes could also constitute a boundary for a child to cross. Clare Rose in *Children's Clothes* (1989) quotes a boy, James Brady, whose day in 1909 was divided between work in the morning and school in the afternoon, and had to wear the appropriate garments for each half: '... change from corduroys and scarf into knicker-bockers and collar and button-on bow ...'. When shorter skirts became fashionable for younger girls in the 19th century, a longer skirt or dress would normally be worn for work unless the nature of the employment made it impractical. Ironically, work garments such as trousers, jerseys and smocks also inspired the clothes reformers of the 1880s and '90s to urge more comfortable clothes for children, initially those of the middle classes who would not have to earn a living until their teens, if at all. They were also the basis for some of the best-known weatherproof garments, such as the (shepherd's) sheepskin coat and (fisherman's) oilskins.

dates from ancient times onward.

derivation descriptive.

wrapper a long, loose-fitting garment, sometimes with a crossover front, serving as a compromise between a dress and a dressing gown, for wear in the house. As such it was also typically worn constantly by invalids and convalescents, and in its later form tended to be quite substantial, possibly with this usage in mind. In Susan Coolidge's novel *What Katy Did* (set in the mid-1860s), cousin Helen sends a crimson wrapper for Katy (aged about twelve) to wear when she is housebound after an accident. In a childhood context, the word was also used less precisely to describe a shawl or similar covering.

dates 18th century to about 1914 (towards the end of this period, more typical of the USA).

derivation from the action of wrapping it around the body.

Wrapper
Cotton
British, 1820–40
V&A: Misc.4–1982

wrapping gown a long, fairly loose day gown worn by babies and young children, wrapping over in front and often accompanied by a sash round the waist; possibly, like the *jummer*, inspired by Asian dress.

dates 1700–1800.

derivation descriptive.

yarmulke see *kippah*

Opposite
Wrapping gown
Printed cotton
British, *c.*1750
V&A: T.879–1919

Pasolds Ltd, Ladybird
brand catalogue
illustration of Y-fronts
Printed paper
British, 1976
V&A: MoC

Y-fronts™ short, close-fitting underpants with cut-away legs for men and boys, the centre front seams shaped like an inverted letter Y. They were considered particularly suitable for boys, probably because of the ease of removal and repositioning (compared with boxer shorts and other similar garments) when dressing and using the lavatory. They probably also appealed to boys because the later versions at least tended to be available in bright colours and patterns, whereas the more traditional underpants were generally white, cream or other neutral colours.

dates 1953 onward.

derivation from the Y-shaped front seam; it was originally a trade name originated by the Scottish firm Lyle & Scott, but as the construction was widely copied by other manufacturers, *Y-fronts* quickly became a generic term for the garment.

youth movement uniforms see *Appendix 2*

08/10. Boy's Brief. Knitted 85% Cotton minimum. Machine Wash.
Colour: 6/12 solid, Turq **17,** Gold **55.**
Height: 92cm 104cm 116cm 128cm
Code: **02** **04** **06** **08**
Height: 140cm 152cm
Code: **10** **12**

zephyr a small square shawl of lightweight fabric; also applied to other lightweight fabrics and garments.

dates 1820s–1930s. 'Zephyr frocks and knickers for the children' (Selfridges Bargain basement advertisement in *The Star*, 9 April 1930); 'Striped zephyr' shirts for boys (Army & Navy Stores catalogue, 1939–40).

derivation from *zephyr*, a gentle breeze, in reference to the garment's or fabric's light weight.

zouave jacket a short jacket with rounded front corners and a single fastening at the neck. Rather than becoming part of a 'zouave suit', the boys' version of the jacket was used both singly and in many different types of suit. It occurs particularly in those based on historical styles, possibly because it was seen as containing few features that would tie it to a particular period.

dates as a childhood fashion, most characteristic of the 1850s and 1860s, but surviving in boys' suits at least until the 1880s.

derivation from a French army regiment originally formed by members of the Algerian tribe Zouaoua, which had a distinctive uniform.

Selfridges advertisement
for zephyr frocks
Printed paper
British, 1930
V&A: MoC

Samuel Brothers,
zouave jacket
Velveteen
British, 1880–90
V&A: T.186–1930

Appendix 1

Layettes

The layette was supposed to contain everything needed for the clothing (and in some cases care) of the newborn child for the first few months of life. In 1700 there might be a simple list of basic requirements to help the mother prepare for the birth: swaddling bands and garments, and other helpful items such as candles and soap. During the 19th century, the whole concept became more complex, and acquired the French name 'layette'. Some of the longest and most prescriptive lists date from the 1930s, but rationing during the Second World War enforced a return to a more basic approach. Layette lists are seldom found after the 1990s, and current versions are phrased in terms of helpful suggestions rather than a 'must-have' list.

These lists preserve the spellings of the originals.

1742

Cap
Biggin
Forehead-Cloth
Head-Cloth
Long-Stay
Bibb
Frock
Upper coat
Petticoat
Bodice-Coat
Barrow
Mantle
Sleeves
Blanket
Neckcloth
Roller
Bed
Waistcoat
Shirt
Clout
Pilch
Stockings
Shoes

Foundling Hospital Checklists for recording
clothes worn by children, generally no more
than one year old on arrival.

1759

Ribbons
Cap
Bonnet
Biggin
Forehead-Cloth
Head-Cloth
Long-Stay
Bibb
Gown
Frock
Upper-Coat
Petticoat
Bodice-Coat
Robe
Barrow
Mantle
Sleeves
Blanket
Neckcloth
Handkerchief
Cloak
Roller
Bed
Waistcoat
Shirt
Clout
Pilch
Stockings
Shoes

1843

4 nightgowns	3 whittles**
4 first-sized day caps	6 first-sized shirts
5 long robes	2 flannel caps
4 day gowns	2 short chemises
for first month	Baby linen, basket
8 pinafores	and cover
2 dozen napkins	Powder box
3 flannel barrows*	Pincushion***
9 back wrappers	Feather for bed,
4 flannel belts	and blanket
or soft calico binders	Soft sponge and soft
	brush for the hair

* barracoats
** white baby garments of various types, in this case
  said to be shawls
*** ordinary pins were still much used to fasten baby clothes

Cunnington family correspondence of 1843, quoted by
Phyllis Cunnington and Catherine Lucas in *Costume
for Births, Marriages and Deaths* (1972).

1870

Belly-bands [preferably flannel]
Napkins [tie-on for preference]
Shirts
Loose dresses
Cloak, spencer and shawl for outdoor wear
No caps except out of doors
No pins, or as few as possible [patent safety pins
  are mentioned]
Nothing tight, or longer than a little
  beyond the feet
Shortening at two to three months depending
  on the time of year

Pye Henry Chavasse, *Advice to a Mother* (1870).

1885

6 lawn shirts
4 night gowns
4 muslin monthly gowns
3 muslin robes
2 cambric slips
2 Saxony day blankets
2 night blankets
3 flannel pilches
2 flannel bands
2 linen bands
2 head flannels
2 monthly boots
6 bibs
24 linen diapers

Advertisement for Mrs W.B. Proctor's Ladies' and Baby Linen Warehouse, *Myra's Journal* (1 May 1885).

1902

4 binders of unhemmed flannel
4 woollen vests [knitted or woven, short-sleeved in summer, long in winter]
4 flannel blankets [worn like barracoat]
4 monthly gowns [for use during day and night] [flannel or cashmere, yoked and long sleeved]
2 day gowns [flannel or cashmere, yoked and long sleeved]
Knitted stockings
4 dozen Turkish towelling nappies
Flannel squares to cover nappies
4 pilches
2 head flannels [indoor use for moving child from one room to another only]
2 knitted woollen hoods [outdoor use]
1 large woollen shawl

Ada Ballin, *From Cradle to School* (1902).

1936 [to make]

4 woollen vests (bought or home-knitted)
4 nightgowns
4 flannel petticoats
4 dresses (daygowns)
1 large carrying shawl (bought or crocheted)
2 to 3 dozen Turkish towelling napkins (bought ready-made)
3 pairs of bootees (knitted)
1 sleeping bag (for the pram)
2 bonnets (or crochet caps)
2 matinee coats
1 or more silk or muslin robes, with nainsook petticoats to wear beneath
This last item is not essential … but … most mothers like to include just one (or perhaps two) …

Agnes Miall, *Making Clothes for Children* (1936).

1936 [to buy]

6 wrap over vests
4 long flannels (barracoats)
4 long petticoats
6 day gowns
6 cotton nightgowns
2 (Chilprufe brand) nightgowns
6 nun's veiling* nightgowns
2 robes (long dresses) – muslin, organdie or net
6 hand-knitted wool jackets
1 crepe de chine shawl
1 wool carrying shawl
2 light Shetland (wool) shawls

1 silk matinée jacket
6 bibs of hand-embroidered muslin
3 dozen Turkish (towelling) squares
3 dozen (Harrington's brand) squares
2 pairs cot blankets
6 linen pillowslips
6 embroidered muslin pillowslips
1 down quilt – plain or floral
Organdie cot-trimmings
Cane basket

* a soft, lightweight wool

The Harvey Layette, Harvey Nichols Catalogue (1936).

1947

2 flannel binders*
3 or 4 silk-wool or
   knitted wrapover
   vests
3 long slips
3 barracoats
   [sometimes omitted]
4 cotton nightgowns
4 day gowns
1 wool bonnet

2 dozen Terry
   towelling diapers
2 dozen gauze squares
1 house shawl,
   36" square
1 wool carrying
   shawl
2 wool coatees or
   matinée coats
2 pairs wool bootees

Mittens are illustrated but not listed.

No pins or buttons
Shortening at about three months … Many
mothers will have nothing to do with long
clothes for babies. They prefer to put babies
straight way into short clothes.

* Approx 6 x 18". When the navel is healed, substitute
flannel bands with shoulder straps for binders.

Elizabeth Craig, *Elizabeth Craig's Needlecraft*
(1947, revised edition).

c.1950s

4 vests
2 day barracoats*
2 night barracoats*
3 petticoats
3 nightgowns
3 day gowns
3 woollen coats
2 matinée coats

4 pilches
18 towelling napkins
3 pairs of bootees
3 pairs of mittens
2 bonnets or caps
2 shawls
1 head shawl

Gone are the 'long clothes' in which our
mothers took so much pride. Those weighty and
cumbersome garments are to-day considered
very unhygienic. The aim in baby clothes is to
have them light, warm, roomy, and just about
27 inches long.

Trimmings must be simple … no elaborate
embroidery is advisable.

* 'This garment is sometimes omitted from the layette'
– but detailed instructions and illustrations are given
for two distinct styles, one modern and one traditional
(pp.346–52).

Sarah G. Service & Agnes B. Laird, *The Big Book of
Needlecraft* (undated).

1956

Layette recommended for the first
three months [long clothes]

4 nightgowns   bonnet and mitts
1 or 2 day gowns   for a winter baby
4 wrap-over vests   2 doz. Turkish
2 petticoats for wear   napkins
   under thin frocks   2 dozen muslin
2 head shawls   napkins
   30" square   or patent pilch
2 carrying shawls   and pads [instead
   60" square   of napkins]
4 pairs bootees   6 bibs
2 to 4 matinée coats   6 handkerchiefs
                                 1 crepe bandage to
                                    make 3 binders

For shortening [short clothes, for four months onward]
3 or more frocks or romper suits
2 petticoats to wear under thin frocks
4 vests second size
4 or more pilches
4 pairs socks
baby shoes and bootees
large feeders
2 or more second size matinée coats or cardigans
pram set: coat, leggings, bonnet, mitts
larger nightgowns or sleeping-suits when required

M.F. Hepworth, *How to Make Nursery Clothes* (1956)

1969/70

3 infant nightgowns   3 babystretch [stretch
3 vests   suit] for night or day
2 packets [of 12]   2 pairs mittens
   terry nappies   3 bonnets
1 packet [of 12]   3 pairs bootees
   gauze nappies   3 matinee jackets
2 packets of 3   2 baby's first blankets
   Ever-Dri* nappies   [usable as shawl]
3 plastic pants

*one-way filter nappy for wear next to the skin

Mothercare catalogue 1969/70

Appendix 2

Youth Movement Uniforms and Styles of Dress

Beaver Scouts The youngest group
of Scouts, for those aged between six and
eight years, was founded in 1986. They wear
turquoise sweatshirts (polo shirts in summer)
with a Scout neckerchief and navy blue or other
dark trousers, socks and shoes.

Blue Birds From 1913, girls younger than
eleven could belong to a junior movement of
Camp Fire called Blue Birds, and wore the
middy blouse with a blue beret and skirt that
the older girls wore for informal occasions.

Boys' Brigade, Boys' Life Brigade

The Boys' Brigade was founded by William
Smith in 1883. The movement has always
had a deliberate policy of minimal uniform
cost, in order to be as inclusive as possible.
To begin with, members simply wore a red
rosette to show that they belonged to the
movement. In 1884 they began adopting
uniform items, initially a soft cap, which in
1885 changed to a belt, stiff cap and haversack
(pouch), all worn with their own clothes.
In Scottish groups the Glengarry bonnet
was often worn as the hat. The next major
change was the use of various special (and
much more military) uniforms: the Boys'
Brigade Scout uniform, in use between 1909
and 1927, was more like that of the Scout
movement, with Scout-style shirt, hat etc.;
between 1918 and 1923 companies could join
the Territorial Force Association, and wore
khaki service tunics, breeches and puttees (an
alternative version, between 1919 and 1932,
was in grey).

Founded in 1899, the Boys' Life Brigade had
many similar aims and attitudes to the Boys'
Brigade, including one of minimal uniform to
begin with. They wore forage caps at first, but
were early in adopting the field service cap,
which by 1918 they were wearing with a navy
blue 'tunic shirt' piped in magenta, a lanyard,
magenta tie and navy shorts (or military style
breeches with puttees for the over-fourteens).

In 1926 these two movements merged.
The cross of the Boys' Life Brigade was
combined with the anchor of the Boys' Brigade
for badges and other insignia. Members
continued to wear 'Uniform A' (Boys' Brigade)
and 'Uniform B' (Boys' Life Brigade) until 1930.
At this point the whole movement changed
to a uniform of navy shirts with blue ties,
navy shorts, a black or brown belt and black
stockings with two white rings, which
remained the basic form. From 1967 'ordinary
clothing' was an option for the senior boys,
and from 1971 blue jerseys with grey shorts
for the younger ones. New field service caps
in lightweight synthetic fabrics were adopted
in 1970.

Boy Scouts, Scouts The Scouts were

founded by Robert Baden-Powell, following on
from the experimental camp for boys, which he
held on Brownsea Island in 1907. The original
Scout uniform consisted of a shirt in blue,
khaki, green or grey, worn with blue or khaki
shorts, a neckerchief in the troop's colour, a
brown leather belt, a khaki hat with a wide
brim and a chin strap, and tabbed knee-length
socks in khaki or other dark colour with black
or brown shoes. The Scout also carried a staff
marked in feet and inches. The characteristic
woggle (neck scarf ring) worn by Scouts was
introduced in the early 1920s: an article
'Wear a Scarf Woggle' appeared in *The Scout*
magazine on 9 June 1923. The origin of the
word seems to be unknown.

Apart from the replacement of the hat with the
beret in the 1950s, and the option of grey shorts
introduced at the same time, Scout uniform
remained remarkably constant over the years,
until the 1967 Working Party introduced green
berets, green long-sleeved shirts and long
mushroom-coloured trousers, retaining the
belt, scarf and woggle. Meg Andrew redesigned
Scout uniform (taking effect from 2003) with
a far larger range of colours and garments
including fleeces, sweatshirts and 'activity'

trousers as well as more formal garments. Scouts now wear teal blue shirts and navy trousers, with scarf and woggle. The modern category of Explorer Scouts (aged fourteen to eighteen) wear beige shirts with navy trousers and the scarf and woggle.

The Scout movement also includes Air Scouts and Sea Scouts. The first Air Scout Patrol was formed in 1935, and the uniform was a blue shirt, shorts and cap with the usual neckerchief and woggle. The Air Scouts were formally founded as a group in January 1941, with a uniform of light blue shirt and grey trousers, and were the first Scouts to wear a beret instead of a hat.

The Sea Scouts began in 1908, and wore similar uniform to Boy Scouts, but with a navy blue jersey and shorts, a neckerchief and woggle, and a round hat like a naval rating's. They still wear a hat or cap, a navy blue jersey with black or navy trousers and optional belt, and a lanyard.

As with the Scout movement in general, the uniform of both groups now includes a number of other options such as fleeces, waterproof jackets and sweatshirts.

Brownies Brownies (the junior version of Guides and originally known as Rosebuds), for girls aged from seven to ten, started in 1914. It was customary to wear a dark blue jersey and skirt with a tammy hat, and a promise badge. In 1915 a tie was added and the further option of a brown dress with a straw hat, and in 1916 a brown belt was added to the blue outfit. A brown tunic dress with breast pockets and a brown or navy tie and knitted hat were introduced in 1917. Brown knee-length socks, already in unofficial use, were added as an official option in 1929. A brown summer uniform with a cloth cap was introduced in 1934, and the pale gold-coloured tie as an option in 1938 (but all the pack had

to wear the same colour). A brown wool beret was introduced in 1950 instead of the cloth cap, and a brown cardigan in 1964. The cotton dress was redesigned with pockets in the skirt in 1967, and there was also a new promise badge and yellow crossover tie. A knitted bobble hat took the place of the beret in 1973, and brown trousers were allowed for wear beneath the dress in 1977.

A completely new uniform, designed by Jeff Banks, was launched in 1990, with yellow or brown sweatshirts, yellow T-shirt, brown shorts or culottes or sweatpants, a brown sash to carry the badges, a new promise badge and an optional baseball cap.

Another new uniform appeared in 2002, designed by Ally Capellino, with hooded jackets, leggings, gilets, skirts and T-shirts.

Camp Fire (later **Camp Fire USA**)

Luther H. and Charlotte V. Gulick started the Camp Fire movement for girls of eleven and over in 1910 in the USA; the UK movement followed in 1921. It encourages many of the same practical skills as the Guide and Scout movements, and tests its members in a similar way but within a quite different framework. Camp Fire was based on a romantic version of Native American culture, with each member originally making her own ceremonial costume based on the dress of the squaw, and choosing herself a new name for her identity within the group. The royal blue border of the Camp Fire membership pin bore the three elements of the word 'Wohelo' in silver: 'Wo' for work, 'he' for health and 'lo' for love, still one of the key philosophies of the movement (the Wohelo medallion, later the Wohelo Award, is now the movement's highest honour).

For informal occasions each girl had a middy (sailor style) blouse with a blue beret and skirt, but the important item was the ceremonial gown for special occasions. The gown was issued plain, and had to be decorated in a way unique to its wearer (with every piece of decoration required to have meaning). Regulations also stipulated dark knickers (no petticoat), with dark stockings and moccasins or dark shoes on the feet. A triangular badge on the breast of the gown carried the emblem of the camp to which the wearer belonged. The coloured wooden beads attached to it were 'Honours', awarded for seven crafts: orange (home craft), red (health), brown (camp craft), green (hand craft), blue (nature craft), yellow (business craft), red/ white/ blue (citizenship). Larger beads, known as 'Big Honours', were for achieving a group of honours in a craft. A string of ten purple beads was also awarded for each rank attained. Runner was the basic rank on joining. The more senior ranks rose through Wood Gatherer, who wore a silver ring decorated with a bundle of seven silver faggots symbolising the seven points of the law: seek beauty; give service; pursue knowledge; be trustworthy; hold on to health; glorify work; be happy. Next, the Fire Maker had a silver bracelet with the word 'Wohelo' around it in Tsimshian Indian characters. The most senior, Torch Bearer, wore a silver pin quartered to represent the four seasons, with the wearer's own device plus the rising sun, the lightning flash in the shape of the 'W' of 'Wohelo', and the pine tree.

Campfire expanded to include boys in its membership in 1975, and the ranks (and their requirements) have been re-created: Little Stars, Starflight, Adventure, Discovery, Horizon, Teens in Action. Uniform and recognition items are still worn, but are mainly in the form of white polo shirts and T-shirts with coloured waistcoats, and various emblems and badges.

(Girl) Guides

The first Guides appeared, unofficially, in 1908: they adapted Scout uniform, wearing a khaki or green skirt with a khaki blouse and hat. On being officially formed for girls between ten and fourteen in 1909, the uniform colour was originally a company decision, but had been resolved as blue by 1911. The uniform consisted of a dark blue blouse with breast pockets, a dark blue skirt, a hat and a blue tie. Some changes were made to the skirt length and blouse pockets in 1917, a belt was added, with a yellow tie instead of a blue one, but the next major change was the introduction of a blue dress in 1930, although the skirt and blouse remained an option. In 1946, the uniform changed back to a blue blouse and navy skirt, with a beret. The beret was replaced with an 'air-hostess' hat in 1964. At the same time, the style of the blouse and tie changed, and skirt lengths fluctuated in accordance with fashion. In 1981, a neckerchief replaced the tie.

Like the Brownies, the Guides had designer makeovers by Jeff Banks and Ally Capellino in 1990 and 2000 respectively. Banks designed a flexible mix-and-match group of garments including a jumper, polo shirt, sweatshirt, skirt and trousers in bright blue and navy, with a sash for badges earned. Capellino's version includes a gilet (which carries the badges), rugby shirt, and sweatshirt in dark and mid-blue with red.

Girls' Brigade

An amalgam, formed in the mid-1960s, of the Girls' Brigade (Ireland) (founded 1893 in Dublin), the Girls' Guildry (Scotland, 1900) and the Girls' Life Brigade (England, 1902), all organizations with similar aims and simple uniforms, like the Guildry Maids' plain navy skirts with white blouses and red sashes. Its ranks originally consisted of Cadets (6- to 9-year-olds), Juniors (9 –12), Seniors (12 –14) and Pioneers (14 and over). The current ranks are Explorers (under 8), Juniors (8 –10), Seniors (11 –13) and Brigaders (14 –18). The formal uniform is based on a white shirt and navy tunic for the younger two groups and white shirt and navy skirt for the older two; the informal version consists of navy tracksuit bottoms, white blouse and navy sweatshirt.

Lifeboys The Lifeboys were the junior section of the Boys' Life Brigade, and were founded in 1920. Their first uniform was a saxe blue jersey with dark blue shorts and peaked cap. In 1927 they adopted a round naval hat worn with a blue jersey and shorts, subsequently changing details such as lettering on hat bands. As part of the BLB, they also merged with the Boys' Brigade in 1926.

Rainbows The group was started in 1987 as a junior version of Brownies, for girls aged between three and seven. Members wear tabards in six of the seven rainbow colours (red, orange, yellow, green, blue and violet), originally with an optional green cap. From 2004 they have had the additional option of red jackets, jogging pants and cycling shorts (all with pale blue trim), red caps and pale blue polo shirts.

Rangers The older age range of Guides was originally (1916) called Cadets and wore Guide uniform with a white hat badge and band, and a white tie. In 1920 they became Rangers, with a red badge and hat badge (Sea Rangers wore similar navy uniform to Sea Scouts but with skirts). Ranger uniform colour changed to blue in 1939 with a navy hat and red badge, and in 1942 they changed again to a grey jersey with a navy skirt, tie and beret (still with red badge). In the 1950s other approaches were tried, including a battledress blouse and a suit, but the next major changes came in 1967 when all branches of Rangers merged as Ranger Guides, whose uniform was an aquamarine blouse and navy skirt and cap, with the option of a navy pinafore dress in 1975. Jeff Banks's redesign in 1990 gave them further aquamarine-coloured garments, including sweatshirts and polo shirts, and Ally Capellino kept the aquamarine theme in 2002 for various shirts and tops, with a navy cap and grey jacket.

Wolf Cubs, **Cub Scouts** The junior version of the Scouts was founded in 1916 for boys under the age of eleven. The original uniform consisted of a green jersey, dark shorts, a neck scarf and woggle, a yellow corded green cap and tabbed socks. The age range is now from eight to ten and a half. The modern uniform is a green sweatshirt with dark trousers and a neck scarf and woggle.

Woodcraft Folk Founded in 1925, this is a progressive educational movement which has no uniform as such. Its website explains, 'our members choose to wear clothing such as our "woodie hoodies" or t-shirts designed by young people from our organisation'. The movement has always emphasized the environment and the skills required to live within it, and the role of young members (its first leader, Leslie Paul, was 19); it has strong links to the peace movement and the cooperative movement. Currently, members are called Woodchips (under 6), Elfins (6–9), Pioneers (10–12), Venturers (13–15) and District Fellows, or DFs (older teenagers and adults).

Most youth movement uniform items were almost impossible to come by during the clothes rationing of the Second World War.

Most of these groups now admit both boys and girls, so the uniforms often include an optional skirt or trousers.

Appendix 3

What Went Underneath

Early 18th-century baby

 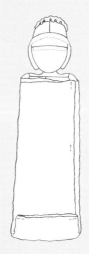 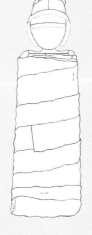 

Layer 1
Forehead cloth with shirt and nappy

Layer 2
Add cap and blanket or 'bed'

Layer 3
Add swaddling bands

Layer 4
Add decorative outer swaddling band (optional)

18th-century boy

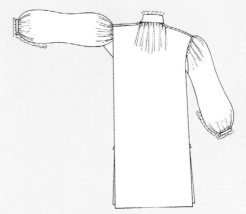

Front
Shirt (long enough to be tucked between legs as substitute for underpants)

Back

18th-century girl

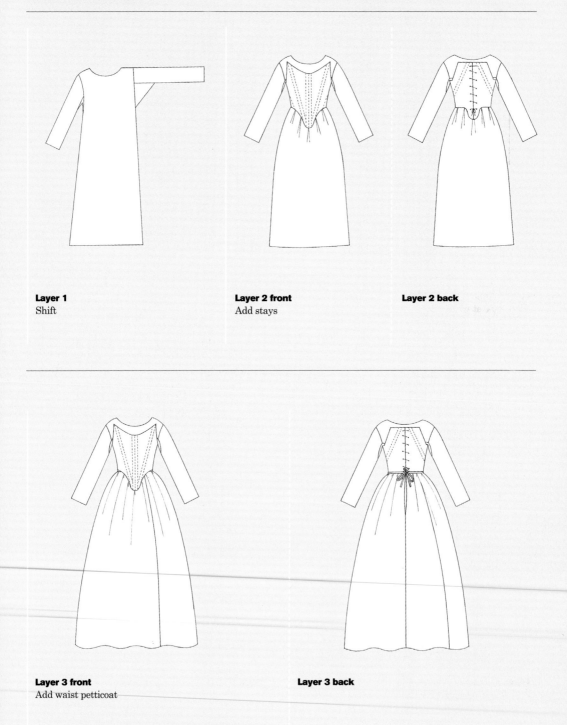

Layer 1
Shift

Layer 2 front
Add stays

Layer 2 back

Layer 3 front
Add waist petticoat

Layer 3 back

Layer 4 front
Add petticoat with bodice

Layer 4 back

Layer 5 front
Add underskirt and pocket

Layer 5 back

19th-century baby (c.1880)

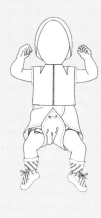

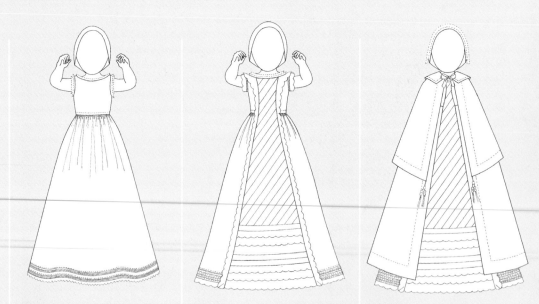

Layer 1
Binder, nappy
and shirt

Layer 2
Add cap, pilch
and bootees

Layer 3 front
Add barracoat

Layer 3 back

Layer 4
Add petticoat
with bodice

Layer 5
Add long gown

Layer 6
Add cape and bonnet

19th-century boy (c.1850)

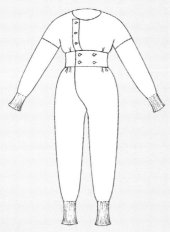

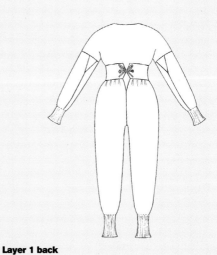

Layer 1 front
Undershirt and long
underpants

Layer 1 back

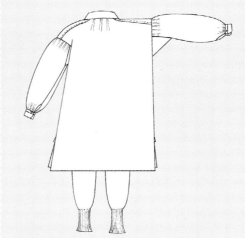

Layer 2 front
Shirt

Layer 2 back

19th-century girl (c.1840)

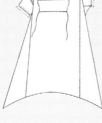

Layer 1 front
Chemise

Layer 1 back

Layer 2 front
Add corset

Layer 2 back

Layer 3 front
Add drawers (and tuck
chemise into them or
leave loose)

Layer 3 back

Layer 4 front
Add petticoat
with a bodice

Layer 4 back

20th-century baby (1950s)

Layer 1
Nappy

Layer 2
Add waterproof pants

Layer 3
Add vest

Layer 4
Add petticoat

Layer 5
Add dress

Layer 6
Add knitted bonnet,
coat and bootees

20th-century boy (1920s–1940s)

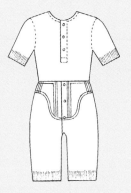

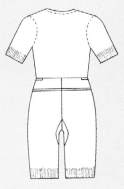

Front
Vest and underpants

Back

20th-century girl (1920s–1950s)

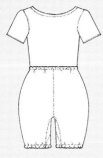

Layer 1 front
Vest and knickers

Layer 1 back

Layer 2 front
Add liberty bodice

Layer 2 back

Layer 3 front
Add petticoat

Layer 3 back

Appendix 4

Typology

This section is to help the reader who is unfamiliar with clothing terminology. It contains the names of garments, and is divided into those for babies and toddlers, and those for children. The terms are further divided into garments for similar purposes, and within these categories into groups of similar garments or those worn on the same parts of the body.

Babies' & Toddlers' Clothes

Underwear and nightclothes

bapkin
disposable (nappy)
gauze square
knapkenette
muslin square
nappy
nappy liner
reusable (nappy)
tailclout
pilch, pilcher
trainer, training pants
bed
binder, bellyband
body belt
liberty bodice
roller
stayband
staybodice
swathe, sweather
chemise
first shirt
vest
barracoat (barricoat,
   barrow, barrow
   coat, pinning
   blanket, robe
   blanket, etc.)
flannel
petticoat
nightgown
baby bag
ear cap
scratch mitten

Outer clothing

angel top
cardigan
matinee coat or jacket
shrug
babygro

babystretch
buster suit
romper suit, rompers
stretch suit
dress
frock
gown
mantle
   (pre-19th century)
robe
slip
wrapping gown
tights
swaddling/swathing
   bands or clothes
long stay

Accessories

backstring
leading strings
reins
bib
dribble catcher
feeder
muckinder,
   muckinger (and
   other similar
   words)
biggin
bonnet
cap
caul
crosscloth
forehead cloth
pudding, black
   pudding
infantee
mitten
sleeves
boot, bootee
shoe
sock
slipper
nappy pin
pins, pincushion
safety pin

Outdoor clothes, etc.

baby bunting
bearing cloth
blanket
bunting
carrying cape
cloak
hug-me-tight
mantle (19th century)
palm
pelerine
pram set
shawl
whittle
zephyr
leggings, legginettes

Occasions

bearing cloth
chrisom
Christening gown/
   clothes/robes
Circumcision gown/
   clothes/robes
palm
receiver
short coating,
   shortening,
   tucking up

Children's Clothes

Underwear and nightclothes

chemise, shimmy
semmit
shift
shirt (originally)
   singlet
smock (originally)
   undershirt
vest
bandeau

bra, brassiere
busk
corset(s), corselette
foundation garment
roll-on
stays
training bra
camisole
chemisette
liberty bodice,
   utility bodice
petticoat bodice
cami-knickers,
   camiknickers,
   camiknicks
combinations
bloomers
boxer shorts, boxers
briefs
directoire knickers
drawers
g-string
knickers
knicker linings
leglets
long johns
pantalettes
pantaloons
pants
thong
trowsers
trunks, trunk
   drawers
underpants
V-string
Y-fronts
bustle, dress
   improver
crinoline, crinoline
   petticoat
hoop, hooped
   petticoat
petticoat
slip (girls), bra-slip
bunny top
clock

garter
hamster sock
hose, hosiery
pop sock
sock
stocking
suspender
suspender belt,
   garter belt
tights, pantyhose
toe sock

baby doll pyjamas
pajamas
pajamarette
pyjamas
sleep suit
sleeping vest
nightdress
nightgown
nightshirt
banyan
bed-jacket
dressing gown
housecoat
kimono
shrug
wrapper
bed sock
mob cap
nightcap

Outer clothing
(upper torso)
blouse
bolero
boob tube
cardigan
cheat
chemisette
habit shirt
jersey, guernsey
jumper
middy blouse
pullover
shirt
sweater

sweatshirt, sweat
T-shirt, tee shirt
tank top
twin set
waist
waistcoat (US vest)
woollie, wooly
(lower torso, bifurcated)
bell-bottoms,
   bell-bottom trousers
breeches,
   knee breeches,
   buckskin breeches
camouflage trousers
capri pants
cargo trousers
chinos
combat/kombat
   trousers
cords, corduroys
culottes
divided skirt
drainpipes
flares
hot pants
jeans, denims
knickerbockers
lederhosen
leggings
loons
oval trousers
palazzo pants
pantaloons
pedal pushers
plus fours
   (also plus twos)
skort
slacks
toreador pants
trews
trousers
ufo trousers
(lower torso, skirted)
apron
kilt
ra-ra skirt

skirt
skort
(whole torso, bifurcated)
air-raid suit
bubblesuit
catsuit
dungarees
Eton suit, Etons
Fauntleroy suit,
   Little Lord
   Fauntleroy suit
flying suit
jack tar suit
jumpsuit
man-o'-war suit
pinafore suit
play slacks
Russian suit
sailor suit
siren suit
skeleton suit
sun suit
(whole torso, skirted)
cassock
djibbah, jibbah
dress
dust wrapper, etc.
fishwife dress
frock
gabrielle dress
gown
gymslip
Highland suit
jubbah
jummer
kaftan, caftan
mantua
overall
pelisse robe
pinafore, pincloth,
   pinner
pinafore dress
princess dress
robe
saccarine
sundress

surplice
Russian suit
sack, sack-back,
   sacque
sailor suit/dress
Scotch suit
sister frocks
smock
tabard
tunic
washing frock

Styles and genres
aesthetic clothing
Bloomer
charity uniform
costume
evening dresss
Fair Isle knitwear
garibaldi jacket,
   shirt, etc.
gender indicators
hand-me-downs
hussar dress
Kate Greenaway
   dress/style
L-85
orthopaedic garments
party clothes
school uniform
suit
Sunday best
toe the line
traditional and
   superstitious items
uniform (youth
   organizations,
   school, etc.)
Utility garment/
   scheme/wear
Vandyke dress/
   clothing
working clothes

Coats, jackets, protection from the weather, etc.

anorak
blazer
blouson
bomber jacket
coat
convoy coat
duffel/duffle coat
fishtail parka
fleece
gilet
greatcoat
hacking jacket
hoodie
Inverness cape/
   cloak/coat
jigger coat
kagoule, cagoule
furs
jacket
lumber jacket
mac, mack,
   mackintosh
manteau
Nehru jacket
Norfolk jacket
overcoat
paletot
parka
pea coat/jacket
pelerine
pelisse
raincoat
reefer jacket
sac(k), sacque
shearling coat
snorkel, snorkel coat/
   jacket/parka
spencer
swagger coat
swing coat
tow coat
ulster, ulsterette

waterproof,
   waterproof coat
windcheater
zouave jacket

burnoose, burnous
cape
cloak, gipsy cloak
mantle
poncho
sarape, serape
tippet

bosom friend
comforter, muffler,
   scarf, ruff
leg warmers
shawl
spat, spatterdash
parasol, sunshade
umbrella
walking stick

comfi suit
lumber suit
pixie suit
snowsuit, snow bunny
sou'wester
sunbonnet
sunglasses
sunhat

clog
galosh
gumboot
patten
rubber
snow heel
wellington boot

Head and neck, chest and waist

alice band
bandeau
deely bobbers/boppers
disco headband
feely boppers
hairband
(hair)grip
(hair)slide
kirby grip
scrunchie, scrunchy
snood

baboushka
balaclava, balaclava
   helmet/cap
baseball cap
beanie hat
beret
bicorne hat
biggin
boater
bobble cap/hat
bonnet
bowler, bowler hat
breton hat
cap
coif
cloche
curtain
deerstalker
derby hat
ear cap
ear muff
fontange
forage cap
glengarry bonnet
(head)scarf
kippah
koppel
hat
lappet
leading strings
mob cap
panama, panama hat
pixie hood/cap

pompadour
pompon
pudding, black
   pudding
quartered cap
riding hood
sou'wester
sunbonnet
tam-o'-shanter,
   tammy, tammie
top hat, topper
topknot
trappa kap
tricorne
veil
yarmulka, yarmulke

bow tie
choker
collar
Eton collar
falling collar
lanyard
neckerchief
Peter Pan collar
tie
tucker

basque, basque
   waistband
belt
brace
fichu
leading string
pocket
sash
snake belt
swiss belt
waist belt

Hand, wrist and arm

armlet
cuff
glove
handkerchief,
   hankie, hanky
mitten
muckinder,
   mockateer, etc.
muff
muffatee, muffetee
sleeve

Foot

boot
bronze shoe/
   boot/sandal
Chelsea boot
Dr Martens,
   Doc Martens, DMs
gaiter
galosh, golosh
gum-boot, gumboot
jodhpur boot
kamak
mukluk, muk
pixie boot
rubber
ugg
wellie, welly,
   wellington boot,
   wellington
clog
patten
brogue
cromwell
derby
Derby jail boot
loafer
mary jane
moccasin
oxford
pump
shoe
slipper

winklepicker
flashlight trainer
heely
streetglider
trainer, training shoe
beach shoe
flip-flop
jelly
mule
plimsoll
sand shoe
sandal
slipper
sneaker
surf shoe
veldtschoen sandal

Sport/leisure

bathing dress/
   costume
bikini
swimming costume,
   swimsuit
tankini
trunks
waders
wet suit
football strip
hacking jacket
jodhpurs
jodhpur boot
knickerbockers
flashlight trainer
gymshoe
leotard
plimsoll
shell suit
shorts
singlet
tracksuit
trainers
shorts
salopette(s)
sunglasses
sunsuit, sundress
T-shirt, tee shirt

Occasions

Bar/Bat Mitzvah
   outfits
First Communion/
   Confirmation
   outfits
bridesmaid dress
flower girl dress
pageboy suit
ring-bearer suit
evening dress
party clothes
Davy Crockett hat/
   shirt/outfit
dressing-up clothes
fancy dress
Montem costume
picture dress
armband
mourning,
   half mourning
shroud

Select
Bibliography

A Lady, *The Workwoman's Guide*
(*c.*1838; reprint London, 1986)

Ballin, Ada S., *The Science of Dress*
(London, 1885)

Buck, Anne, *Clothes & the Child*
(Bedford, 1996)

———, *Costume in the Eighteenth Century*
(London, 1979)

Cassell's Household Guide (London, 1870)

Cunnington, P., and Buck, A., *Children's
Costume in England 1300–1900* (London, 1965)

Cunnington, C.W., Cunnington, P., and Beard,
C., *A Dictionary of English Costume*
(London, 1960)

Cunnington, P., and Lucas, C., *Charity
Costumes* (London, 1978)

———, *Costume for Births, Marriages and
Deaths* (London, 1972)

Cunnington, P. and Mansfield, A., *English
Costume for Sports and Recreation*
(London, 1969)

Ewing, Elizabeth *History of Children's Costume*
(London, 1977)

———, *Dress and Undress* (London, 1978)

Forrester, Wendy, *Great-Grandmama's Weekly*
(Guildford and London, 1980)

Guppy, Alice, *Children's Clothes 1939–1970*
(Poole, 1978)

Haddon, Celia, *Great Days and Jolly Days*
(London, 1977)

Hitching, Wilena, *Baby-Clothing on Healthful,
Economical & Original Lines*
(London and Edinburgh, 1914)

Holt, Ardern, *Fancy Dresses Described, or What
to Wear at Fancy Balls* (London, 1887)

Hughes, M.V., *A London Family in the 1890s*
(Oxford, 1979)

Laver, James, *A Concise History of Costume*
(London, 1969)

Lurie, Alison, *The Language of Clothes*
(Feltham, 1983)

Martin, Linda, *The Way We Wore*
(New York, 1978)

Olian, JoAnne (ed.), *Children's Fashions
1860–1912: 1065 Costume Designs from 'La
Mode Illustrée'* (New York, 1994)

Page, Christopher, *Foundations of Fashion*
(Leicester, 1981)

Pasold, Eric W., *Ladybird Ladybird*
(Manchester, 1977)

Phillips, John Page, *Children on Brasses*
(London, 1970)

Picken, Mary Brooks, *A Dictionary of Costume
and Fashion* (New York, 1985)

Rose, Clare, *Children's Clothes* (London, 1989)

Rutt, Richard, *A History of Hand Knitting*
(London, 1987)

Swann, June, *Shoes* (London, 1982)

Toomer, Heather, *Baby Wore White*
(Radstock, 2004)

Walkley, C., and Foster, V., *Crinolines and Crimping Irons* (London, 1978)

Walkley, Christina, *Welcome, Sweet Babe, a Book of Christenings* (London, 1987)

Waller, Jane (ed.), *Some Things for the Children* (London, 1974)

Sources

Alcott, Louisa M., *An Old Fashioned Girl* (1870; most recent reprint Rockland, MD, 2007)

——, *Eight Cousins* (1875; most recent reprint Rockland, MD, 2007)

Anonymous, *The New Female Instructor* (London, originally published 1834; republished 1988)

——, *Domestic Economy: A Class-Book for Girls* (London, 1897)

Army & Navy Stores General Price List, 1939–40 (London, 1939)

Austen, Jane, *Mansfield Park* (1814; most recent reprint Oxford, 2008)

Barrie, J.M., *Peter Pan* (1904; reprinted London, 1988)

Brazil, Angela, *My Own Schooldays* (London, 1927)

——, *Ruth of St Ronan's* (London, 1927)

Brent-Dyer, Elinor M., *Seven Scamps* (London, 1927)

Briggs, Julia, *A Woman of Passion: The Life of E. Nesbit* (Penguin Books, 1989)

Brittain, Vera, *Testament of Youth* (1933; London, 1978 reprint)

Brontë, Charlotte, *Jane Eyre* (1847; most recent reprint Oxford, 2008)

Bryson, Bill, *The Life and Times of the Thunderbolt Kid* (London, 2007)

Burnett, Frances Hodgson, *Little Lord Fauntleroy* (1886; most recent reprint Charleston, SC, 2007)

Burnett, T.A.J., *The Rise and Fall of a Regency Dandy* (London, 1981)

Burns, Robert, *Tam O' Shanter* (1790; most recent reprint Darvel, Ayreshire, 1992)

Cadogan, Dr W., *A Letter to one of the Governors of the Foundling Hospital, by a Physician* (London, 1748)

Carroll, Lewis, *Through the Looking Glass and what Alice Found There* (1871) in Gardner, Martin (ed.), *The Annotated Alice* (Penguin, 1977)

Chavasse, Pye Henry, *Advice to a Mother* (London, 1870)

Collins, Andrew, *Where Did It All Go Right?* (London, 2003)

Coolidge, Susan, *What Katy Did* (1872; most recent reprint Teddington, 2007)

——, *What Katy Did at School* (1873, most recent reprint Teddington, 2007)

Cooper, Jilly, *Class* (London, 1997)

Cooper, Thomas *Thesaurus linguæ Romanæ et Brittanicæ* (1565; cited thus in OED Online at http://dictionary.oed.com via Borough Library Services)

Craig, Elizabeth, *Elizabeth Craig's Needlecraft* (London, 1947)

Dean, Heather (ed.), *The Winter Book for Girls* (London, 1956)

Dickens, Charles, *The Life and Adventures of Nicholas Nickleby* (1839; most recent reprint Charleston, SC, 2008)

——, *David Copperfield* (1850; most recent reprint Oxford, 2008)

——, *Dombey and Son* (1848; most recent reprint Oxford, 2008)

——, *Oliver Twist* (1838; most recent reprint Oxford, 2008)

——, *Sketches by Boz* (1836; London, 1907 reprint)

Dyche, T., and Pardon, W., *A New General English Dictionary* (1735, cited in OED Online at http://dictionary.oed.com via Borough Library Services)

Edgeworth, Maria, 'Eton Montem', from *The Parent's Assistant*, vol.6, online text at www.archive.org, 2008)

Farjeon, Eleanor, *A Nursery in the Nineties* (Oxford, 1980)

Forest, Antonia, *Peter's Room* (London, 1961)

Forsyth, H., with Egan, G., *Toys, Trifles & Trinkets* (London, 2005)

Fulford, R. (ed.), *Dearest Child: Letters between Queen Victoria and the Princess Royal 1858–1861* (London, 1964)

Gandy, Ida, *Staying with the Aunts* (London, 1963)

Garnett, Eve, *The Family from One End Street* (Harmondsworth, 1971)

——, *Holiday at the Dew Drop Inn* (Harmondsworth, 1971)

Gaskell, Mrs, *Cranford* (1853; London, 1964 reprint)

Hughes, Thomas, *Tom Brown's Schooldays* (1857; most recent reprint Teddington, 2006)

Irving, Washington, *History of New York* (1809, cited in OED Online, at http://dictionary.oed.com via Borough Library Services)

Joubert, Laurent, *Popular Errors* (1578; English translation Tuscaloosa, 1989)

Kerr, Rose, *The Story of the Girl Guides* (London, 1942)

Lewis, C.S., *The Last Battle* (1956; Harmondsworth, 1966 reprint)

MacCarthy, Fiona, *Eric Gill* (London, 1989)

Marshall, Alfred, *The Interlinear Greek-English New Testament: The Nestle Greek Text with a Literal English Translation* (London, 1958)

Milne, A.A., *Winnie-the-Pooh* (1926; London, 1966 reprint)

Oxford English Dictionary (Oxford, 1989 and Additions 1993 and 1997)

Pardoe, M., *Bunkle Began It* (London, 1942)

——, M., *Bunkle Butts In* (London, 1943)

Pares, Winifred, *The Secret of the Dusty House* (London, undated)

Pollock, Linda, *A Lasting Relationship* (London, 1987)

Powell, Anthony, *A Question of Upbringing*
(Book 1 of *A Dance to the Music of Time*)
(London, 1951)

Pryor, Felix (ed.), *The Faber Book of Letters*
(London, 1988)

Raverat, Gwen, *Period Piece* (London, 1954)

Rousseau, Jean Jacques, *Emile* (1762; London,
1969 reprint)

Rowe, Wm and & Co. Ltd, *The Royal Navy
of England and the Story of the Sailor Suit*
(Gosport & London, *c.*1900)

St Denis or Dionis Backchurch, parish register
(1572; published London 1882)

Streatfeild, Noel, *Ballet Shoes* (London, 1936)

———, *Curtain Up* (London, 1944)

———, *Gran-Nannie* (London, 1975)

——— (ed.), *The Years of Grace* (London, 1950)

Thompson, Flora, *Lark Rise to Candleford*
(Oxford, 1979)

Warner, Sylvia Townsend, *Scenes of Childhood*
(London, 1981)

Acknowledgements

My particular thanks to Diane Lees, Director of the V&A Museum of Childhood
(who got this project started) and my other V&A colleagues present and past, especially
Elizabeth Aslin, Pip Barnard, Catherine Bornet, Clare Browne, Anthony Burton,
David Coachworth, Janet Davies, Edwina Ehrman, Alison Fielding, Madeleine
Ginsburg, Peter Glenn, Caroline Goodfellow, Avril Hart, Wendy Hefford, Audrey Hill,
Catherine Howell, Ken Jackson, Lucy Johnstone, Marion Kite, Sue Laurence, Tina
Levy, Esther Lutman, Barbara Morris, Rob Moye, Stephen Nicholls, Geoff Opie,
Halina Pasierbska, Natalie Rothstein, Samantha Safer, Suzanne Smith, Sonnet Stanfill,
Imogen Stewart, Abraham Thomas, Lucy Tindle, Veronica Tonge, Vanessa Trevelyan
and Sarah Louise Wood.

A heartfelt thank you to Mark Eastment, Asha Savjani and Monica Woods for
encouragement and help, Ali McConnachie at Holmes Wood who deserves a medal for
fitting it all together, and my copy editor David Hallworth and project editor Johanna
Stephenson, both of whom have shown astonishing patience and meticulousness.

Everyone who has donated garments to or otherwise helped with the building up of the
V&A's collection of children's clothing, and to the students and researchers who flagged
up the need for this book.

The many other costume historians, curators and experts who have shared their
knowledge, books and enthusiasm over the years, including Mary Alexander, Anne
Buck, Gill Clark, Leonie Davis, Patric Dickinson (Richmond Herald), Hazel Forsyth,
John Heyes, Susan Hutchings, Anthea Jarvis, Amelia Johanson, Andrew Mackay,
Valerie Mansfield, Joanna Marschner, Kathy McMakin, Martha Pullen, Clare Rose,
Roberta Stok, Fiona Strodder, June Swann, Joan Wayman, Judy Wentworth,
Gillian White and Maggie Wood.

My family, especially Keith Marshall, and my cousins Janet Brown, Mary Richardson,
and Jane Salter, and friends, particularly Maeve Orr and Jill Weekes, all of whom have
been extremely patient and supportive while my attention has been elsewhere.

Copyright Credits